I0868164

on track ...

Rush

1973-1982

every album, every song

Richard James

SONICBOND

sonicbondpublishing.com

Sonicbond Publishing Limited
www.sonicbondpublishing.co.uk
Email: info@sonicbondpublishing.co.uk

First Published in the United Kingdom 2024
First Published in the United States 2024

British Library Cataloguing in Publication Data:
A Catalogue record for this book is available from the British Library

ISBN 978-1-78952-338-6

Typeset in ITC Garamond Std & ITC Avant Garde Gothic
Printed and bound in England

Graphic design and typesetting: Full Moon Media

Follow us on social media:
Twitter: https://twitter.com/SonicbondP
Instagram: www.instagram.com/sonicbondpublishing_/
Facebook: www.facebook.com/SonicbondPublishing/

Linktree QR code:

on track ...

Rush

1973-1982

every album, every song

Richard James

SONICBOND

sonicbondpublishing.com

Acknowledgements

My thanks are due to the following people:

Mike Rawsthorne, for reading everything I write and agreeing with me most of the time; Alison James, for explaining the long words and reminding me why grammar is important; Dotty Trippier, for being my best guitar student and introducing me to the music of McFly.

on track ...

Rush 1973-1982

Contents

Enter Stage Left ...

Some school friendships last a lifetime. Bands formed in teenage years, however, rarely last into adulthood. If they do, any form of success is unusual. This puts Gershon Eliezer Weinrib and Aleksandar Živojinović in a unique position. Add in, slightly later, Neil Ellwood Peart, and you have a highly potent, exceptionally talented, progressive heavy rock trio, which would be eventually awarded the Order of Canada and be included in the Rock 'n' Roll Hall of Fame. In short, Rush.

The trio would become musical heroes to a massive fan base with statistics that may amaze those unfamiliar with their work. Over 43 million album sales, promoted by over 2000 concerts; a five-decade career; 20 studio and 11 live albums, and some of the best rock music ever recorded, is an unmatched record for a band which, with one early exception, maintained the same line up throughout their career. In terms of album sales alone, Rush are only bested by The Beatles (four members) and The Rolling Stones (five members). So, from a mathematical standpoint alone, they offer the highest ratio of talent per player to quantifiable success. Numbers and statistics really matter to some people. For the trio from Ontario, not so much. They just wanted to play the music they wanted to play, their way or not at all. It was only and always the music that mattered. Everything that followed (fame, fortune and occasional despair) was merely a consequence of doing what they were best at, a fact that many legions of fans across the globe can attest to.

This book reviews the band's output from their debut album in 1974 to 1982's *Signals* – a pivotal album that saw the trio immerse themselves more and more in the prevailing musical trends of the period (New Wave, ska, and reggae). *Signals* was also the final album that long-term producer and unofficial fourth man Terry Brown would work on with the band. I refer to the incarnation of the band with John Rutsey as Rush 1.0 and his seminal replacement with Neil Peart as Rush 2.0.

Becoming one of the most successful power trios in the history of rock was not bad work for three adolescents who saw themselves as outsiders in their teenage Toronto suburbs, finding solace, focus, and a future in music. And even with all their accumulated fame and fortune, Lee, Lifeson, and Peart never felt part of the mainstream, revelling in being regarded as the 'world's largest cult band'. As musicians, Rush have enjoyed enormous respect and have consistently appeared at the top of critics' lists for their instrumental mastery. They have been nominated for 35 Juno Awards; they were Canada's 'Group of the Decade' in the 1980s and were named 'Musicians of the Millennium' by the Harvard Lampoon, the satirical magazine; a joke that the band were happy to receive as a foil to their perceived seriousness.

Weinrib (Lee) and Zivojinovic (Lifeson) met at Fisherville Junior High, in the Willowdale district of Toronto. They bonded over jokes, sports and especially music. In a 2016 interview with *Classic Rock* magazine, Alex remembered that they became best friends, while Geddy recalled:

> We were sons of Eastern European immigrants who had left Europe after the Second World War to start a new life in Canada. So we were both a little bit different. My parents were Polish Jews, survivors of the Holocaust. They met when they were thirteen at a work camp, and they were both in Auschwitz for a time. My mom had such a strong Jewish accent, which is how I ended up being known as Geddy instead of Gary, my real name and basically, it stuck.

Alex continued:

> I'm a first-generation Canadian. Both my parents were Serbian. They actually met in Canada after the war. They had come over as refugees. My father had been married before, to a Serbian woman. They had married in Italy, and my sister was born there. They tried to get into the States, but they were denied and then sent to Canada. In cities like Toronto, they didn't really want these people, but Eastern Europeans could find work in the mines in British Columbia, and my mother's family worked on a farm. My father's first wife died, and some years later, he met my mother. We eventually moved to Toronto in the early 50s because there were greater opportunities there.

Across the road from the Lifeson family lived the Rutseys, and Alex befriended their son, John. Geddy and Alex soon acquired guitars and jammed together at school. Afterwards, they would frequently go their separate ways with Alex playing music with John, who had a set of drums. Alex and Geddy would perform together occasionally, especially after Geddy acquired an amplifier. Rutsey and Lifeson formed a band called The Projection, with Jeff Jones on bass and vocals. It was Bill Rutsey, John's brother, who suggested a name change to Rush. By the spring of 1968, Geddy, too, had joined his first band, a loan from his mother securing him his first bass.

In September 1968, Rush were offered a regular, paid gig on Friday nights at The Coff-In, a coffee bar in a church basement. While Rutsey and Lifeson were excited by the development, Jones didn't share their enthusiasm and didn't show up for the show. Alex called Geddy to fill in, and after a short rehearsal, he joined the band. It was also at The Coff-In that the band was noticed by a young promoter-to-be, Ray Danniels. In the *Classic Rock* interview, Geddy remembered:

> I was a pretty shy kid. I didn't really want to be a frontman. I was just the one with the best voice – or the most appropriate voice! So, stepping out in front was not a natural thing for me. I had to learn how to deal with it. John used to announce the songs, and he was totally good at it, really funny, a real acerbic wit. And in those early days, John was the leader of the band, to all intents and purposes. He was a very opinionated guy – about music, about what he thought the band should be, how we should look.

In Martin Popoff's book *Contents Under Pressure*, Alex gave an insight into the band's earliest gigs:

> We knew maybe seven or eight songs – mostly Cream and Hendrix – and we would just play them over and over, repeatedly throughout the night. And through the rest of the week, we would get together and rehearse and learn more songs. We started writing right from the beginning. And we continued doing that gig pretty much on a weekly basis until the spring of 1969. The first gig we played there, there were probably 30 people. By that spring, there were about 200, 250 people. The place was packed. And we had two solid sets of material, and that was a real treat; it was so exciting. We got ten bucks for that first gig. And by the spring, we were getting 35 bucks a week, so it was quite a big increase. Then we started playing high school dances, other drop-in centres, things like that. We continued doing that for the most part until '71, I guess when they lowered the drinking age to 18. And then, all of a sudden, there were all these bars you could play in.

The band started to write as much original material as they could, slotting new creations into their sets, which were otherwise dominated by the music of Led Zeppelin, Cream, Jimi Hendrix and The Who. In the *Classic Rock* interview, Alex noted:

> It was a really great training period for us. At first, the gigs were indifferent, not much interest, maybe a dozen people. But the better that we got at it, we started to develop a following. Word spread, and we became a good draw. After a year of playing clubs, the shows were packed.

Danniels volunteered to be the band's manager. Bookings flowed in, and rehearsals, repertoire, and equipment increased. The musical emphasis shifted from the blues-rock stylings of Cream to the heavier side of the Led Zeppelin sound, with Lee adapting his singing style accordingly. Lyric writing for the band's growing repertoire of original material fell to Rutsey as neither Lee nor Lifeson were confident in their ability as wordsmiths. Belief in their songwriting grew with more of their own songs featuring in gigs, although Rutsey was less enthusiastic about the developing musical direction preferred by Lifeson and Lee.

Rush decided to turn professional. Soon, they were gigging most nights of the week, although venues reacted less favourably when they played at excessive volume or performed their own unknown compositions. By the end of 1971, they had a regular gig at the Abbey Road pub, which paid $1,000 a time. This meant an investment in better equipment and transportation.

By the end of 1972, the band's reputation was building. Hard work on the live circuit ensured an expanding fan base, the balance between cover songs and original material was shifting still further, and they had enough material to record an album. A lengthy demo tape was sent to Canadian record companies, who summarily rejected the trio. Unrepentant, they continued with regular gigging.

In early 1973, Danniels joined forces with another promoter, Vic Wilson, to form SRO (Standing Room Only) Productions. Danniels and Wilson encouraged the band to release a single and created their own record label, Moon Records. Fearing that Rush's own compositions might not be the winning hand to play, the band were persuaded to cover the Buddy Holly song 'Not Fade Away', with an original tune, 'You Can't Fight It' as the B-side. These were recorded at Eastern Sound Studios in Toronto under the clueless direction of David Stock.

A few hundred copies were pressed, with Danniels going into promotional overdrive with record companies and radio stations, all to no avail. The single vanished into rightful obscurity, with the remaining copies being sold at a loss at gigs. The first time I heard these songs was thanks to a recording placed on YouTube. The single has never been formally re-released or added as a bonus track to a CD, which, in all honesty, we should all be thankful for.

Not Fade Away Single

'Not Fade Away' (Norman Petty/Charles Hardin) (3.15)

Buddy Holly's famous song from 1957 gets an early mauling, the band taking inspiration for their performance from The Rolling Stones' own cover version of the track released in 1964.

The vocals? Well, the word 'helium' springs to mind. Lee's double-tracked voice sounds just plain weird in the context of this famous song. It's easy to understand why this version of the band struggled to secure a record deal. As a piece of Rush history 'Not Fade Away' is an interesting curio, but it does nothing at all to suggest future glories. The recorded sound is weak and underpowered; Rutsey sounds like he is playing on shoe boxes, and while the guitar has some excellent power-chord moments, the bass merely burbles away in the background. This cover of a cover of a classic pop hit goes on for too long, illustrated by a curious 'vocals only' section at 2.10. This is where it should have stopped, but then we are at least treated to an early example of Lifeson's talent with a bluesy, distorted guitar solo in the overly long play-out.

'You Can't Fight It' (Lee/Rutsey) (2.52)

This is, strangely, more like it, but only given that 'Not Fade Away' is such a low bar to get over. 'You Can't Fight It' is an energetic bluesy composition with an interesting 'heavy country' opening riff and Lee sounding more like, well, *himself.* Rutsey has some decent drum fills in the chorus, and Lifeson throws in another impressive solo, full of attack and melody. The track comes across as a heavy pop-rock shuffle with plenty of musical ideas allied to some truly dreadful lyrics: 'Rock and roll 'til you lose control. Go down, fall down, not too far'. Despite this terrible handicap, 'You Can't Fight It' is markedly better than the A-side, although the clichéd, big rock ending does it no favours.

In the *Classic Rock* interview, Alex recalled:

> It was a song that people knew and could identify with, rather than an original Rush song. The feeling from management was: let's do something that people will get as an introduction. I think that was bad advice. Playing that song live was great. We played it quite heavy. It sounded really good. But the recorded version was terrible.

In the absence of outside interest, Danniels decided that the band should release an independent album as a calling card. This was recorded in five days, on a very tight budget, at Eastern Sound, with the inexperienced Stock once again behind the desk. By now, Rutsey was feeling pressure from two directions. A diabetes sufferer, the band's punishing schedule was damaging his health, and he wasn't happy with Lifeson's and Lee's emerging and preferred progressive rock direction.

Vic Wilson suggested a fresh pair of hands and ears might perform the required trick. Terry Brown had been an engineer back in the United Kingdom, from where he hailed, before moving to Canada in 1969. With his business partner Douglas Riley, Brown opened Toronto Sound in the same year. SRO provided the funds for a remixing of the songs. Brown also offered a critical ear and suggested that 'Not Fade Away' be dropped in favour of another band original, 'Finding My Way'. 'You Can't Fight It' similarly bit the proverbial studio dust. In *Anthem – Rush In The Seventies*, also by Martin Popoff, Geddy reflected upon the significance of Brown's input and effect on the nascent Rush sound:

> He just had this air of 'I know what's wrong with it, and I know which songs are lousy, which you should drop, and do you have any other songs?' And we threw some songs together and played them, and he picked A, B, and C, and we thought, 'This guy is really cool, this guy knows what he's doing.'
>
> And then we went into his studio and started re-recording some parts and recording the new songs, and they sounded how we wanted them to sound. And we were just so blown away by that; he became the father figure right away. He turned a terrible disaster into something we were proud of – he knew exactly what to do. He was kind of a wizard character to us. We thought he was amazing. He was so nice and so considerate and got the best out of us, and we immediately had this warm feeling about the guy. He became our mentor for a lot of reasons like that. He was always very decisive with us. And he was always so 'This is the right thing to do; this is not the right thing' He had a very responsible attitude towards work, and he would work all hours.

Rush

Personnel:
Geddy Lee: lead vocals, bass
Alex Lifeson: guitars, backing vocals
John Rutsey: drums, percussion, backing vocals
Recording locations:
'Finding My Way', 'Need Some Love' and 'Here Again': Toronto Sound Studios
'Take A Friend' and 'In The Mood': Eastern Sound Studios
'What You're Doing', 'Before And After' and 'Working Man': Eastern Sound Studios, remixed by Terry Brown at Toronto Sound
Released: 1 March 1974 on Moon Records
All tracks by Lee and Lifeson, unless noted
Produced by Rush and Terry Brown
All songs composed by Lee & Lifeson, except 'In The Mood' by Lee
Chart positions: Canada: 86, US: 105, UK: did not chart

Terry Brown knew exactly what he was doing. He captured a far more immediate, aggressive and realistic sound of Rush 1.0 in his studio, and an excited band prepared to unleash their first offering on the world to initially very little effect…

When is a Rush album not a Rush album? *Rush* is the sound of a band, ahem, finding their way. For fans that joined post-Peart, this is the release that doesn't sound 'right'. My own early Rush buying experience went backwards in time, starting with *All The World's A Stage* as a 'taster' and then, once hooked, buying the other four albums in reverse order, as it were. By the time I got to *Rush*, I did wonder whether the right vinyl had been placed in the single sleeve – it was that strange. Only Lee's vocals and the pounding heaviness of Lifeson's guitar convinced me that I hadn't been sold a dud.

Whilst the music is decidedly different to that of the early post-Peart performances, showing strong signs of the band's early influences, the main problem is the lyrics. During pre-recording rehearsals, Rutsey, the main writer, destroyed his work at the last minute. Accounts vary as to why this happened; Rutsey was plagued by bad moods, he had health issues and Lee is on record as believing that Rutsey actually feared success. Whatever the truth, at this crucial stage in the band's career, they had the music but not the words. The job was left to Lee. And it shows. Geddy takes much of the blame and credit for completing this race under pressure.

The cover, a garish affair, was by Paul Weldon. Of course, this being an album which did not have the backing of a major label, the cloth must be cut accordingly. At least the design leaves the purchaser in no doubt as to what they are going to hear; the artwork is as much 'in your face' as the sound is 'in your ears'. Basic, but effective. The now iconic eponymous title logo is bright pink (the original pressing was issued in red), exploding towards us with cartoon-style debris in the background. Designed to portray the music's power and energy, it just looks, unsurprisingly, cheap. On the reverse, the band are shown as individual black and white head-shot rocks flying towards us. Lifeson has a typical 'serious rock' look; Rutsey is, bizarrely, smiling, and Lee wears his best poker face expression. All three are backlit to suggest more power coming from (beneath, between) and behind them.

'Finding My Way' (5.05)

Things get off to a reasonably satisfying, if unspectacular, start. Notable mainly for the distinctive vocals and melodically aggressive guitar work, 'Finding My Way' is a solid lump of four-to-the-floor, early Zeppelin-esque, heavy blues rock.

It fades in with a riff panning left to right in the stereo channels; Lee makes a dramatic appearance with 'Yeah, oh yeah' and continues with the sub-optimal lyrics ('Who am I? I'm coming out to getcha!'), straight out of the Robert Plant playbook. Bass and drums add musical stabs and a steady rhythmic tempo sets in at 0.46. Far away from the lyrical themes which Rush version two would explore, the chorus begins with 'I'm finding, finding my way back home.' Where, exactly, have you been? This conundrum is never resolved.

A second verse and chorus lead into a new 'walking blues' riff at 2.29, a further chorus line, and a first solo for Lifeson, which is played out over the verse chord progression. At 3.37, there is a more interesting instrumental section with some harmonised guitar lines in between Lee's 'Shah!' vocals. Another chorus is followed by a brief repeat of the introduction. Verse one was so good that apparently it is granted a reappearance as the last instalment with a final chorus before the song comes to a tight close.' 'Finding My Way' is a decent opener, but that's all it is.

'Need Some Love' (2.19)

Oh dear. 'I'm running here, I'm running there, I'm looking for a girl' The rest of the first verse gets no better and 'Need Some Love' is a prime example of why record companies heard nothing to electrify the ears when they listened to the album.

This was the first original song to be recorded. According to an interview Lifeson gave to *MusicRadar* in 2011, it was written by Rutsey and Lee, although Lifeson is often credited as Lee's writing partner for the track. Lyrics notwithstanding, 'Need Some Love' is a brisk little blues rocker which slows to a half-time feel for the choruses.

Interest is awakened after the second chorus with a heavy instrumental section (1.22 – 1.50), which features some excellent slide guitar playing and a suitably anguished-sounding, bluesy solo. After the third chorus, this section is briefly repeated, leading to another crisp ending. Unspectacular and mostly disappointing, at least 'Need Some Love' doesn't trouble the ears for too long.

'Take A Friend' (4.24)
If you ever need to organise a rock music trivia pub quiz, have this one on me:

> What's the connection between the 21st-century English pop-rock band McFly and legendary Canadian progressive rockers Rush?

The answer is the opening 30 seconds of McFly's 2023 song 'Land Of The Bees' and the introduction to 'Take A Friend'. They say 'inspired by'; I say 'carbon copy of, with a few extra notes added'. McFly have admitted to a strong liking for Rush's music. Lee and Lifeson have yet to return the compliment. Despite this similarity, the listener's attention is immediately engaged. Oddly, this is the only time, to my limited knowledge, that McFly have incorporated Rush's influence into their music. True, their respective styles are not exactly congruent. True, this is an apparent one-off. Yet, it's an intriguing link between two very different bands.

Okay, beer glasses down, back to the track. Initially, 'Take A Friend' shows real promise. A revolving, rising arpeggio pattern in 6/8 time fades in, adding some interesting parallel fifth and octave harmonies. This first showing of semi-prog inventiveness comes to an end 27 seconds in, as a medium-tempo riff of vaguely Lynyrd Skynyrd-esque proportions lumbers over the horizon and squats over most of the rest of the track.

The chorus has some nicely harmonised vocals, culminating in 'So good!' which a healthy dose of delay has added to it. After a second verse and chorus, Lifeson has a stirring solo despite the restrictions of the underlying chord sequence. By 2.49, it's time for a third verse which maintains the lyrical quality established thus far: 'Yes, you need some advice, so let me put it to you nice.' Another chorus, then a fourth and a fifth (it's not *that* good) verse follow, and then, suddenly, the music takes a savage and unexpected left-hand turn back to the introduction. The arpeggios slow, a lot of reverb is added to the mix, and the track slows to a puzzling, inconclusive close.

In a 2023 interview with Laura Cooney for Entertainment Forum, Danny Jones said "Land Of The Bees' (was) our first ever song that was inspired by Rush. (It) has a 7/4 time signature in it, and if you don't concentrate through that one, you're gonna get lost!'

Seriously, though, give the McFly song a listen. It's really good ... and if you must steal, steal from the best. Yes, Tom Fletcher, I'm looking at you!

'Here Again' (7.34)
Ballad Warning! Slower of speed and more spacious in texture, with some unexpected acoustic guitar behind the verse vocals, 'Here Again' is a welcome change of pace and mood. Again, the blues is strong in this one, with Lee straining at the top of his range, full of emotion as he sings Lifeson's lyrics. There are some beautiful guitar arpeggios washing to and fro in the background, growing ever more powerful. Finally, at the end of the second

verse, the music moves from its minor key (Em) into the relative major (G) for the soaring chorus. This is the best section of the track and the album thus far; it's strong, highly melodic, and possesses an epic stature and power.

At 4.37, Lifeson steps forward for a lengthy, tasteful solo, which makes much use of the space between his notes and phrases to create an impressive atmosphere. Although being firmly rooted in the blues his playing shows plenty of sparks of genuine originality and feel. The lines rise and fall against the underlying chord progression, growing in intensity and complexity but never losing sight of the importance of a melodic structure. At 6.33, the chorus reappears to bring this impressive beast to a close with a final solo over the chorus chord sequence and a slowing to the last chord.

'What You're Doing' (4.22)

'Ladies and Gentlemen, will you please welcome back ... Led Zeppelin!' Well, obviously not, but Jimmy Page could lay fair claim to writing the excellent funk-based riff, which is the backbone of this track. Lee's vocals and lyrics also have echoes of Robert Plant. After markedly derivative first and second verses, things become more interesting at 1.08 with a descending seven-note semitone-based riff with the guitar and bass playing in octaves. Verse three follows, with a guitar solo appearing at 2.03.

Again, individuality raises its worthy head at 2.31, where his repeated descending phrase is matched by some thunderous drumming (this is the first time where Rutsey has sounded like anything more than necessary aural wallpaper), and this idea is repeated at 2.41, and again, very briefly, at 2.50. The repeated, descending semitone riff makes a reappearance before the fourth verse at 3.27, ending with a section of big power chords and some fretboard flurries.

'What You're Doing' has some genuine moments of inspiration, but these are swamped by the band wearing their influences so openly on their sleeves. There's nothing wrong with admiring Led Zeppelin, of course, but 'What You're Doing' has more going for it and would be stronger if Rush's latent creativity was front and centre of the composition.

'In The Mood' (Lee) (3.33)

'And the award for 'Dullest Song on the Debut' goes to ...' Well, it's a close run thing, but 'In The Mood' *just* clinches it. Whether it's the sluggish opening riff, the irritating cowbell, the general lack of genuine rock energy, or the woeful words, there's very little here to raise the pulse rate.

The chorus, while musically strong, is lyrically awful: 'Hey baby, it's a quarter to eight, I feel I'm in the mood. Hey baby, the hour is late, I feel I've got to move.' Without wishing to pick unnecessary, if glaring, holes, 'a quarter to eight' is not, unless you are very elderly or seriously infirm, a late hour. 'In The Mood' is your standard blues-rock stop-gap, and even Lifeson's solo at 1.40 sounds like he is merely playing through the motions, not helped by the underpowered tempo or the overall sense of underachievement in all departments.

Another chorus, a repeat of the main riff, and a final verse including the painful words 'I just want to rock and roll you woman, till the night is done' sets up the 'can't come too soon' ending of a brisk power chord finish.

Bearing in mind this is the 'Terry Brown enhanced' mix, one can only imagine how woeful 'In The Mood' would have sounded if the calloused and clumsy production fingers of David Stock had got to grips with this track. That's one mix I would pay good money *not* to have to listen to.

Strangely, 'In The Mood' would feature in the band's live set for far longer than it should. It's fair enough that during the very early years with Peart, the band would play material from their debut album on stage, but almost any other track from *Rush* would have been a preferable choice. Yes, 'In The Mood' would sound better and more energetic in a live setting (almost any song does), but it's still the low point here.

'Before And After' (5.34)

'Before And After' is two songs in one, each independent of the other. It is also the first song which hints at where Lifeson and Lee had their sights set. The opening part (which lasts until 2.17) is entirely instrumental. It is quite beautiful, with an evocative blend of guitar arpeggios and 'natural' harmonics (the bell-like tones produced by touching a string directly above a fret rather than pressing the string into the guitar fretboard). The music builds until at 1.11 where a distorted guitar develops the chord progression, with Lee taking a more prominent role in the mix. We can hear here Lee's development of the bass as the integral, melodic element of the band's future sound. The music quietens again at 1.48, with a nice interplay between bass and cymbals. The chords grow in power and suddenly, we are into the second song at 2.17.

And it is at this point that all that is good is swiftly undone with the return of the blues-rock sound. There's nothing wrong with this chugging rocker, but this section lacks the creativity and melodic strength of the 'Before' section. The track becomes heavily drum-centric at 3.16 and is helped by a soaring contribution from Lifeson at 3.48. The final verse features the lines 'Now my story's over' and it was at this point when writing my notes for this review I realised I hadn't been paying a blind bit of attention to what the lyrics were about, which speaks volumes. The song reaches an excellent climax with Lee putting his voice under maximum stress for the final rising 'Yeah'!

'Working Man' (7.10)

And here it is! This is the perfect example of saving the very best until the last. 'Working Man' gave the band a foothold on success. It opens with a crushing guitar riff of industrial proportions and ferocity. This introduction alone pushes the majority of the rest of *Rush* into the shade as the track gathers power and proceeds to demolish listeners in its path. Brilliant in its simplicity and epic in its scope, it's easy to see why 'Working Man' became adopted as an anthem, initially in Cleveland, but slowly spreading worldwide with its central, universal refrain: 'It seems to me I could live my life, a lot better than I think I am' finding resonance with millions of wage slaves everywhere.

Lee wrote all of the words to this now-classic song the evening before the vocals were due to be recorded.

The song breaks loose from its verse/chorus/repeat structure at 2.06, going into a lengthy, double-time instrumental section, which is the highlight of the entire album. Here, Lifeson has plenty of space to develop his solo, which builds to a fantastic riff played in octaves with Lee at 3.13. Further individualistic soloing follows with the entire section feeling both simultaneously improvised and tightly arranged. The 'octaves riff' reappears again at 4,34, and at the five-minute mark, the instrumental concludes with some heavy power-chording. This builds back into the main song riff and the final verse, which is a straight repeat of the first time we heard it.

I may be overthinking this, but if the preceding instrumental (which has been played out almost entirely based around E minor represented the 'working day'), then the anticipated next verse could have described the narrator's situation, having completed his relentless slog. Or the instrumental is the narrator letting his hair down at the end of the working day or at a weekend before the seemingly endless repetition of the grind starts up again. Just me? Fair enough.

A vast swathe of power chords brings this instant classic to an end; the music slows as if tired after its exertions, with a country-esque series of accelerating guitar string bends which leads to the 'very-much-of-its-time' big rock ending.

'Working Man' stands head and shoulders above everything else on the album, and whilst the inspirations are clear, it still has more than enough class, individuality and sense of purpose to justify its now 'classic' status. It's probably fair to say that, without this song, the band's future would have been very, very different.

Fly By Night

Personnel:
Alex Lifeson: Electric guitars, six and 12-string acoustic guitars
Geddy Lee: bass guitar, classical guitar, vocals
Neil Peart: drums and percussion
Recorded at Toronto Sound Studios, Toronto
Produced by Rush and Terry Brown
Released: 15 February 1975 on Mercury Records
All music composed by Lee & Lifeson with lyrics by Peart, except where noted
Chart positions: Canada: 9, US: 113, UK: did not chart

After the release of *Rush,* SRO continued to attempt, unsuccessfully, to sign the band to a record label. FM radio, however, proved more receptive. The breakthrough came when Donna Halper, music director for WMMS-FM in Cleveland, heard the album. She was immediately struck by 'Working Man', and the station played it to an instant and positive reaction from listeners.

Before long, almost all of the first 3500 pressings had been shipped to Record Revolution, an import specialist music store in Cleveland. Ira Blacker of the booking and management agency American Talent International (ATI) was impressed enough to send copies to record labels, recommending that they give it a constructive listen. Mercury Records finally signed the band in June 1974. The contract granted Rush complete artistic freedom. Little did Mercury know what they were letting themselves in for. At this 'Pre-Peart-Point', neither did Lifeson or Lee. Mercury, SRO, and ATI began to work Rush overtime. The album was quickly re-pressed and re-released.

Rutsey, however, wasn't as ambitious as his bandmates. All three knew that a crossroads was just over the horizon. Lee and Lifeson were musically joined at the hip; Rutsey was isolated and had issues with his health due to diabetes. Perhaps taking the view that quitting was better than being sacked, Rutsey left, leaving a drummer-sized hole of a problem. In *Contents Under Pressure,* Alex commented on the situation:

> We were placed to do this tour and go to America and all of what that meant, but (John) backed out at the time. Plus he also wasn't really interested in where we wanted to go musically. We wanted to move our music into a more progressive area, and he was more straight-ahead rock 'n' roll, which was more of a cross-section of what we were playing in bars at that time. So it was really time to go our separate directions. We liked to play hard rock as a three-piece, but we wanted it to be more challenging, mostly musically, to ourselves.

A replacement shed builder had to be found, and very, very quickly. Paul Kersey, the drummer with the Sarnia-based rock band Max Webster (who would feature regularly as a support act during Rush's early touring years) was asked to join but declined. Rutsey agreed to play out his notice, honouring some theatre-sized gigs, including support slots for Kiss and ZZ Top. Lee and Lifeson auditioned for replacements, hiring a warehouse in Pickering, eastern Toronto, for two days. The first day's interviewees left them feeling disillusioned. On the second day, Neil Peart walked in.

A perpetual introvert, Peart did not enjoy school life. He refused to compromise his identity to try and fit in. Suffering was a predictable consequence, but this only served to drive him to become even more of a non-conformist. Drumming was his release. In *Rush – Beyond The Lighted Stage,* the documentary DVD released in 2010, he recalled his schooldays:

> Once I got interested in rock bands ... and started to grow my hair a little over my ears and wear bellbottoms, ... and the taunting in the hallways and even the physical abuse out in the smoking area, the constant misfit sense for any kid, especially a sensitive one – it wears you down. So, that's why drumming became an instrument of self-esteem. This was the first time I was admired for anything. And that doubled my fervour for playing drums.

By the age of 15, Peart was playing in public, a hobby his parents fully approved of. He joined his first band, Mumblin' Somethin', and persuaded his father to finance a loan for a proper Rogers drum kit. From that point on, the drums became his all-consuming passion. He would practice for long periods on a daily basis, learning songs and drum techniques by listening to the radio. In the DVD *Classic Albums – 2112 And Moving Pictures,* Neil said:

> Every time I would hear a Bill Bruford or a Phil Collins, it was 'okay, that's how good you have to be now. The benchmark went up so high from the early '60s (where) all you had to do was keep a surf beat and you could get in a band. By the late '60s, you had to be able to play in 7/8; you had to be able to transmit through tempo changes and maybe play some keyboard percussion. This was how good you had to be.

After Mumblin' Somethin' ceased, Neil, still a teenager, joined another established local band, J R Flood. He persuaded his parents to let him quit school and go into music on a full-time basis. J R Flood also allowed Peart to try out his lyric writing skills. In a neat parallel with Lee and Lifeson, Neil was more ambitious than his bandmates. He wanted to be in a band that had a record deal.

By the close of 1971, J R Flood's time in the local limelight was over, and Peart decided to move to London to seek musical success. Armed with his savings, drum kit, and record collection, he crossed the Atlantic, hoping to get a foot in the door of English rock music. Initially playing some minor session work, he eventually joined and toured with English Rose, a London-based rock band, but the experience left him disappointed. He went back to Canada for Christmas and a rethink. On his return to London, he worked in a Carnaby

Street gift shop with jazz music and extensive reading filling his leisure time. During 1972, he continued to seek out new musical opportunities, but with little success. He returned home permanently at Christmas and began working part-time for his father's farm machinery dealership, as well as joining a local blues and covers rock band, Hush. In *Contents Under Pressure,* he remembered:

> I was soon getting disillusioned over there by the music industry, realising it wasn't the way I thought it was. You didn't just get good at the music you loved and became successful. I was shocked, appalled, disappointed, disillusioned, all that. I also made the decision that if I can't make a living playing the music I like, then I'll make a living some other way and still play the music I like. That became the point of honour. So, at that time, when the Rush offer came along in the summer of '74, I was playing part-time in a band in bars and working all day in the family farm equipment business to make a living.

When Vic Wilson turned up at the dealership and asked Neil if he would be interested in auditioning for a nearby band, Rush, Neil jumped at the chance. Rush, after all, had a record deal. Perhaps there was a way that the young man could make his living doing what he loved after all…

The initial impressions on both sides were not promising. Peart's introverted character didn't shout 'progressive heavy rock', and his drum kit was on the small side, not that size matters. For his part, Peart had heard that Rush were little more than Zeppelin clones. Nevertheless, he played his heart out, and a subsequent 'jam' session proved to Lifeson and Lee that he was somebody special. In the *Classic Rock* interview, Alex said:

> We were so blown away by Neil's playing. It was very Keith Moon-like, very active, and he hit his drums so hard. And then, after we'd jammed, we chatted and he was so bright. We connected on many levels. I have to admit that on that first day, I said to Geddy, 'You know, maybe we should still hold out and see who else is out there.' But when we talked again, we were convinced he was the right guy.

Geddy recalled some additional details:

> The first thing that we jammed with Neil in his audition was 'Anthem'. That song was written, for the most part, while John was still in the band. It was very different to any of the songs on the first album – more complex. And Neil coming into the band was a kind of confirming final piece of the puzzle. That was very much where he was at. He liked to play things that were difficult to play, and that was the direction Alex and I were moving in. It had a very catalytic effect.

Peart realised that he had been bruised by his London experiences, and this was a chance to play drums for a band with a record deal and an American tour lined up. Even more importantly, Lifeson and Lee shared his ambition to improve and succeed. Peart officially joined on 29 July 1974, Lee's 21st birthday.

Two weeks later, after intensive rehearsals, the 'new' band went back on tour. Baptisms of fire don't come much hotter than 11,000 rock fans at the Civic Arena in Pittsburgh, Pennsylvania. Rush were the support act for Uriah Heep and Manfred Mann's Earth Band. If Peart was nervous it didn't show in his performance. His arrival and integration into Rush was, of course, utterly transformative; all three felt they could now go in a direction, any direction, that they wanted to. So they did.

A week after the first 'new' Rush gig, the band played the Agora Ballroom, Cleveland, which was broadcast live on WMMS-FM. As the band continued to tour, the music they were creating expanded in style and complexity. Rush appeared on Don Kirshner's *Rock Concert*, broadcast on 10 October 1974, which helped the debut album into the *Billboard* charts. Further exposure via an appearance on ABC Television's *In Concert* series assisted sales, and the tour concluded on Christmas Day 1974, back at the Agora.

The work was paying off. *Rush* had sold over 75,000 copies by the end of the year. What was needed was a follow-up and fast. New material had been written on the road, rehearsed, and polished so that the band felt ready to return to the studio in January 1975. Toronto Sound and Terry Brown were natural choices.

Both Lee and Lifeson were savvy enough to know that lyric writing wasn't their forte or their interest, and the 'new boy' (as Peart would sometimes be referred to right up until the band retired), with his love of books and his eclectic reading interests, seemed an ideal lyric-writing candidate. Peart was, therefore, gently pushed into one of the roles he was born for. His intellect, vocabulary and insights, even at this early stage of the band's eventual planetary domination, were significant and long-lasting.

Travel, excitement, and opportunity are underlying themes of the album. If a record is judged by its cover alone, then *Fly By Night* was going to be a very different beast indeed. The stunning image of a massive owl perched on a snowy landscape at night was painted by Eraldo Carugati, based on an idea by Peart, a keen ornithologist. The band also wanted the cover to feature an aeroplane and the Northern Lights, as the album's working title was Aurora Borealis. On the back of the sleeve, the image continues, with the owl's right wing hanging over the three individual colour photos of Lifeson (moodily looking on from an angle), Peart (straight ahead, serious face), and Lee (more hair than facial features). The inside liner cover included black and white photos of the band, producer Terry Brown, and Howard Ungerleider, the band's lighting designer, pictured amongst Peart's handwritten lyric sheets (not in running order), all laid out on the recording desk. In the *Classic Rock* interview, Geddy said:

> 'Anthem' was a holdover. Pretty much everything else on that album was written fresh. With a lot of the songs on that record, the music came first. But sometimes, Neil would have a lyric and Alex and I would put the music to it. There was also a lot of diversity on *Fly By Night,* much more than on the first album. We wanted each song to show another side to the band.

Fly By Night is a giant leap into a bold new future. Sonic colours abound, from the crushingly heavy power of 'Anthem', 'Beneath, Between And Behind', and 'By-Tor And The Snow Dog', to the moments of sublime beauty ('Rivendell'), strongly melodic rockers (the title track, and 'In The End',) and the lighter acoustic drive of 'Making Memories'. 'Best I Can' is old Rush with a new drummer; Peart's contribution lifts an otherwise mundane rocker into something stronger.

There is much sonic light and shade; the prominent use of steel-strung acoustic and nylon 'classical' guitars add much contrast to the differing song styles. Lifeson's electric sounds are magnificent, with 'the song' always at the centre of his playing. Lee's bass work and sound are instantly impressive, his vocals spanning a far greater range of emotions and ability than was previously suggested. And Peart, both as drummer and lyricist, delivers in spades. His forays into the world of fantasy do not jar with the personal reflections garnered from his travelling. The lyrics are intelligent, erudite, and relatable. The overall impression is of an established, integrated unit knowing what they want to achieve and presenting an original project.

Whilst Rutsey was integral to getting the Rush ball rolling, there is a clear sense that, with Peart on board, the trio now had the potential to become something very special indeed. Listening through to the album again years later, it's this sense of anticipation, excitement and the musical unknown which is so enticing. They were young, they were ambitious, they had worked hard to get where they were and there was absolutely no sense that anything could stop them creatively.

Criticisms are few and far between. 'Best I Can' is a clear leftover from *Rush*, 'Beneath, Between, And Behind' should have occupied more space on the vinyl to further develop its musical and lyrical themes whilst, conversely, 'Rivendell' outstays its welcome. But these qualms pale in comparison to what is achieved. Given the period between Peart's joining and the record's release some seven months later, the album is little short of remarkable. Even now, almost 50 years later, Brown's production sparkles. There is space around the instruments, dynamics and different sound textures flourish, many moods are created, none of the songs sound like any of the others, and yet they all have a unifying style running through them. The overall impression is one of enthusiasm, energy, focused talent and ambition, all distilled into a brisk demonstration of where the band could be going next.

'Anthem' (4.21)

To para-(diddle)-phrase, 'what a difference a drumming lyricist makes'. 'Anthem' encompasses many of the hallmarks of Rush's music of the 1970s: unusual time signatures, guitar and bass playing complex melodies, and elaborate drum fills. It also introduces the lyrical theme for which Rush would become renowned: individualism.

At the time, Peart was influenced by the writing of the Russian-born American author Ayn Rand (1905 – 1982). Rand defected to the United States in 1926 and embraced elements of American society: liberty, individualism, capitalism and the importance of constitutional rights. Peart took some of the themes of her book 'Anthem' and incorporated them into his lyrics. As a result, Lee is now singing slogans: 'live for yourself', 'hold your head above the crowd', and advising people to 'never let anyone tell you that you owe it all to me.' It's a far cry from where they were less than a year earlier.

Filled with self-confidence and benefiting hugely from the rhythmic powerhouse of the 'new boy', something special comes crashing through the speakers immediately. The first part of the introduction is fast, complex, syncopated, and not repeated anywhere else in the song. Some crunchy, rising power chords are followed quickly by a speedy descending minor scale run in 7/8 time, which is played three times. This is repeated five times, with the rising sequence being repeated a further three times.

A pick-scrape (a guitarist's trick where the side of the plectrum is forcibly slid over the string winding from the bridge towards the fretting hand) heralds in the second part of the introduction and the main body of the song. And that's all just in the first 30 seconds.

An octave-based guitar riff swings into action with bass and drums synchronising in a 12/8 rhythm. After all the heaviness and intensity of the opening section, the subsequent verse has a more relaxed feel. Things heavy up for the chorus, climaxing at Lee's astonishing rising vocal of the word 'wrought' where his voice goes into the stratosphere over the secondary riff pattern. A section of stabbed power chords with delay added is played twice as the music moves into its second verse and chorus.

After the second chorus, the song moves into an instrumental section (2.26 – 3.09) with Lifeson bearing down mightily on his wah-wah pedal to excellent effect. When the underlying music incorporates the chorus's chord progression, he doubles his melody in the left and right channels with impressive results.

The 'octave riff' brings us back into a third verse and chorus and a coda section where the stabbed power-chord section is played four times (the third repeat features an impressive assault around the drum kit) through, leading to a tight, triplet-based ending.

'Anthem' is musically complex yet still melodically accessible, lyrically original, and very impressive. This is the sound of the three young men unified in musical purpose. The song is both a superb opener and a statement of intent, a positive sign of things to come, a band on an upward trajectory…

'Best I Can' (3.25) (Lee)

And down again. Delete Peart, reboot Rutsey, and 'Best I Can' is a throwback to the first album. Underpowered both musically and lyrically, the words are wince-inducing. Exhibit 'A' – the first and worst verse: 'Don't give me speeches 'cos they're all so droll, leave me alone and let me rock and roll'. The second verse is no better: 'I just like to please, don't like to tease, I'm easy like that. Don't like long rests I must confess, I'm an impatient cat'. As any owner of a feline knows, cats *do* like long rests.

While Lifeson unleashes another wah-wah enhanced solo (1.46 – 2.30), it's Pearts' inventive, vigorous drumming that impresses the most. Throughout the song, he throws in interesting fills and patterns that raise this otherwise hum-drum composition to a more engaging level.

'Beneath, Between And Behind' (3.01) (Lifeson/Peart)

Now, this is *much* more like it. An urgent sounding, rising chord sequence, aggressive drumming, thoughtful lyrics, and a magnificently anthemic chorus combine to make 'Beneath, Between And Behind' an overlooked gem in Rush's early catalogue. The words were Peart's first foray into lyric writing for his new band.

The chorus is the high point of the song; highly melodic and possessing a punkish level of energy, it's the sound of a band enjoying themselves hugely with an exciting and eloquent composition, covering the birth, history and then-present day of the United States.

A surprisingly simple climbing riff-based instrumental section (1.37 – 2.00) leads into a third verse. The lyrics here are a fine example of Peart's writing skills, turning his sharp eye towards his geographical neighbours: 'The guns replace the plough, facades are tarnished now, the principles have been betrayed. The dream's gone stale, but still, let hope prevail, hope that history's debt won't be repaid.'

My only gripe is that this track is too short. There are some wonderful ideas here which could have been developed further. What they do manage to pack into just three minutes is superb; I'd just like to hear more of it.

'By-Tor & The Snow Dog' (8.37)

In the *Classic Rock* interview, Geddy said:

> The lyrics that Neil wrote for 'By-Tor & The Snow Dog' were very tongue-in-cheek. It was a joke that got out of control. Our manager Ray had two dogs, and Howard Ungerleider, our lighting guy, called them Biter and Snow Dog. So Neil took these two names and created fictional characters, and we turned it into a song.

Alex concurred:

> Neil made it into this really powerful story – a good-versus-evil fantasy piece. And what came out of that was something much bigger than just one song. In terms of song structure, 'By-Tor & The Snow Dog' was the first time that we tried to do a whole multi-part piece of music. It was a pivotal song for the band.

Critics could leap on this, the band's first 'epic' track, with glee. Just the titles of the song's four sections would prompt shrieks of 'pomposity' and 'self-indulgence' from those who didn't 'get it'. Those of us that did just didn't care, as 'By-Tor & The Snow Dog' is wonderful. To us, no other band was making music that sounded as good as this, and if you didn't approve, well, that really was your problem.

Briefly, the plot is this: a demon from hell, By-Tor, attempts to open a portal to the Overworld, whose champion, Snow Dog, defeats him in combat, thus saving the living world from the twilight realm of the dead. The composition consists of four main parts: Verse one, 'At The Tobes Of Hades', features By-Tor. Verse two, 'Across The Styx', introduces The Snowdog. 'Of The Battle' is a lengthy instrumental section, and the song concludes with 'Epilogue', which is the third and final verse.

'Of The Battle' is sub-divided into four sections, with the titles 'Challenge And Defiance', '7/4 War Furore', 'Aftermath' and 'Hymn Of Triumph'. No doubt it helped during the mixing stage to have these different parts individually titled: 'I need a bit more bottom end in the Aftermath, Terry.'

'By-Tor' opened up this listener's imagination. No other band was balancing progressive rock music with such incandescent guitars, driving bass, inventive drumming, and fantastical lyrics, which revealed whole new imaginative vistas. Powerful, clever, escapist, loud, aggressive and atmospheric, it was a track like no other to young ears.

There's no time for mucking about. A brisk drum introduction is immediately followed by the beginning of the fantasy tale. Verses one and two are swiftly dealt with, the scene being set in just over a minute. The stage is now ready set for the centrepiece of the composition, the instrumental battle, which is greeted by an all-mighty 'Yeah!'.

For the first two minutes, the song's tempo is maintained with an intriguing duet between Lifeson's wah-wah enhanced guitar and Lee's heavily distorted bass, representing the two protagonists. Lee's tone was achieved by significantly detuning his bass and adding a Fuzztone pedal to the sound, which was then passed through an Echoplex pedal to add delay into the mix. At 3.06, a new melodic theme is established and developed amidst all this sonic conflict. At 3.30, rhythmic stabs from bass and drums enhance the effect, and at 3.54, a more complex, octave-based riff section is heard; this is the band really showing their prog chops. Each melodic cell is followed by a spectacular burst of drumming ability, with each repeat of the riff getting shorter and shorter until all that remains is a single, huge power chord ending at 4.32.

This drifts into a highly atmospheric section as a violin guitar tone (where the guitar output is set to zero, the 'silent' note is played, and the volume is gradually introduced in an effective impression of a sustained note of a violin) is treated with reverb and delay to create a beautiful, mysterious effect. Subtle bass and sparse percussive touches add to the mood. Lifeson changes his contribution from single notes to more substantial chords, and the music grows with greater drum and percussion activity, moving from a fragile state to one of great strength.

A stunning drum roll (to which a phase effect has been added) ushers in the next part of the instrumental, which is a more traditional guitar solo over a guitar, bass and drum backing at a slow tempo in 4/4 time. A final short, rising melody with staccato percussive slabs and the last verse arrives with the results of the match: By-Tor is defeated, and the 'lands of the Overworld are saved again'. 'Again'? So, this has happened before, then? The track ends with the sound of snow crystals, which were etched into the run-off groove on the vinyl release. They would ring out endlessly until the needle was removed from the record. Perhaps the story isn't over…? After all, the world loves a sequel. With one track on the band's next album, this would come to pass. Sort of.

Yes, with the passing of time and the addition of some (optional) maturity, Peart's fantasy tale, and the pretentious titling of this, the album's longest track may come across as trite and ridiculous. But this is to miss the point. Nearly five decades later, 'By-Tor' still holds up. Rush were showing their true colours and the seemingly limitless possibilities of what they could produce. All three musicians contribute equally, with space around the music and an excellent production showing just what could be achieved.

The imagination and complexity of the track was a revelation to a teenage rock fan and while 'By-Tor' was the only song on *Fly By Night* to, ahem, stretch its wings thus far, it hinted at where the band may be heading in the future. It was intoxicating stuff because fans hadn't heard *anything* like this before; it was new and genuinely exciting. This fantastic fantasy is played with precision and *brio,* and there's nothing wrong with escapism when the mood calls.

'Fly By Night' (3.21) (Lee/Peart)

A 'road' song, if ever there was one, there is a lighter, more optimistic feel to the album's title track, enhanced by its major key, optimistic lyrics, and a catchy refrain. Lifeson's solo after the second chorus again shows his skill in playing what fits the song best rather than just careering up and down the fretboard for its own sake. After a third chorus, the track changes direction as a new, more pensive and thoughtful section begins: 'Start a new chapter…'

Peart must, at this point, have been reflecting on his time in London. Subtle guitar arpeggios and light playing on the bass and percussion increase the introspective mood here. At 2.35, confidence returns for the fourth chorus with the repeated lines, 'My ship isn't coming and I just can't pretend'. The last chorus has these lyrics repeated thrice before the song comes to a final, sustained chord.

'Fly By Night' is an excellent example of Rush's ability to write a short, catchy, and memorable rock song with commercial undertones and, as such, it makes a fine title track.

'Making Memories' (2.57)

Another song from the road, but 'Making Memories' doesn't fare as well, mainly due to its less convincing lyrics: 'There's a time for livin' as high as we can, behind us you will only see our dust' and 'Well from sea to shining sea, and a hundred points between, still we go on digging every show' being the chief offenders. The chorus, however, speaks to the overall optimistic mood of the song and the album in general: 'You know we're having good days, and we hope they're going to last. Our future still looks brighter than our past. We feel no need to worry, no reason to be sad. Our memories remind us maybe road life's not so bad.'

Continuing on the positive side, we have an enthusiastically strummed acoustic guitar, some excellent hi-hat playing coming in with the second verse, and Lifeson excelling himself with a wonderful slide solo after the third verse. The play-out section overstays its welcome with Lee riffing his way around the words as Lifeson adds numerous fills and the song fades away. Sadly, 'Making Memories' is unexceptional and is second only to 'Best I Can' as the most underwhelming track on the album.

'Rivendell' (4.57) (Lee/Peart)

An overly long oddity 'Rivendell' is notable for its limited instrumentation (a nylon-strung, classical guitar, Lifeson's atmospheric 'violined' electric guitar backing) and the first appearance of Lee's 'soft' singing voice. The combination is dreamlike and hypnotic, and it is in keeping with the intimate, Tolkein-inspired words. The ambient mood is very effective, and 'Rivendell' does show an unexpected but welcome facet to Rush's songwriting abilities and ambitions.

Fundamentally, the song consists of an introduction, a verse, and a separate section. The fact that this is stretched out over nearly five minutes means the material, good though it is, is spread too thin to maintain interest. If two minutes had been trimmed off it, 'Rivendell' would be a much more involving composition. As it is, it's a relief when the final track hoves into view, and the album springs into life again.

'In The End' (6.46) (Lee/Lifeson)

Another 'Pre-Peart' piece, 'In The End' opens with a beautifully recorded 12-string acoustic guitar chord sequence and the continuation of Lee's gentle voice, maintaining the tranquil mood established with 'Rivendell'. Some cymbal washes and gentle bass are added to the opening verse. The lyrics are personal, unspecific, and universal. The words are aligned with the relatively straightforward music to great effect.

The introduction is repeated and the music comes to a pause. The sustained pitch rises quietly with some clever studio trickery, and then a strident electric guitar heralds the return of the power trio at 1.43. Lifeson adds some superb, syncopated octave melody notes above this powerful rhythm, instantly increasing the power and conviction. Pulsing bass and percussion drive the main, much heavier body of the song, along with the second verse benefiting from Lee's rock voice soaring over the majestic chord progressions.

Lifeson throws in another mature and impressive solo at 4.00. Once again, he doesn't over-reach or try to play an inappropriate phrase or fill. There is a real skill in playing a solo that works for the song, and the guitarist is already demonstrating his mastery of this art.

The mood quietens at 5.41 with a return to the acoustic introduction and the pleasing addition of some clean electric guitar tones. Lee retains his rock voice for the final lyrics, backed by some tasteful bass and percussive fills. The song comes to a close with a final chord and a cymbal swell.

'In The End' is, after 'Rivendell', the most straightforward song on the album, but this does not diminish its power and effect. The dynamic contrasts are effective, nobody is overplaying, and the song just rides out on its own momentum, providing an effective closer to a second 'debut', which, in the main, promises much with the formation of the classic lineup.

With this track, Rush are presenting another stripped-down version of their compositional talents, and the song does not suffer one iota from such simplicity. The song is another demonstration of the breadth of talent and ambition within the band. 'In The End' has an epic quality to it, but it is not trying to ape 'By-Tor's complexity; it is a simple statement delivered with concise and consummate musicianship. This 'new' Rush could clearly write and play in a wide variety of styles within the heavy rock genre, and it was clear that this was only the beginning. They could go in whatever direction they wanted. So they did.

In *Contents Under Pressure*, Neil had his own recollections of this period:

> We just played what we liked. We were always that organic, and still are, through all those changes. There was no 'Let's synthesise these two styles; if we take that element and combine it with this element, we'll have something new.' It was nothing like that. We were never that self-aware, let alone that calculating. It was simply an organic response to playing what we liked. We liked to play loud and energetically, and this new, complicated, sophisticated approach appealed as well.

Caress Of Steel

Personnel:
Alex Lifeson: electric guitars, 6- and 12-string acoustic guitars
Geddy Lee: bass guitars, classical guitars, all vocals
Neil Peart: percussion
Recorded at Toronto Sound Studios, Toronto
Produced by Rush and Terry Brown
Released: 24 September 1975 on Mercury Records
All music composed by Lee & Lifeson, with lyrics by Peart
Chart positions: Canada: 60, US: 148, UK: did not chart

Fly By Night peaked at number 113 in the United States charts. There were two ways to ensure that the next album bettered that – airplay and touring. Unfortunately, the radio stations hadn't heard mainstream commercial rock on *Fly By Night,* a situation that its follow-up would do nothing to alter. Rush concentrated on option two. The mantra seemed to be 'Tour everywhere and anywhere with everybody and anybody.'

On 25 April 1975, they opened for Kiss in front of 4500 people at the Detroit Michigan Palace. They also played as support for Blue Oyster Cult and Aerosmith. Gradually, headline bookings started to appear. The hard work was reaping results, especially when they won the coveted Canadian Juno award for 'Most Promising Band'. By the end of the tour, Rush was regularly selling out 4000-seat venues, and on 27 June, they played at the Massey Hall, Toronto, with fellow Canadian band Max Webster as support.

While they toured new musical ideas occurred and were rehearsed for the next album. In mid-July, Toronto Sound and Terry Brown once again played host. Again, time was tight with the album being completed within an allotted twelve days, the candle being constantly burned at both ends.

Enter stage left Hugh Syme. Syme was the keyboard player with another SRO signing, the now-forgotten Ian Thomas Band. He was also a graphic artist of considerable talent and, at Danniels's suggestion, submitted a pencil-drawn design as the illustration for the cover. Featuring the Necromancer on the front and the Fountain of Lamneth on the rear, his idea was taken and subsequently mutilated by the record company, who added a metallic surround and a sepia tone. The cover art was supposed to be printed with silver 'steel-like' ink, Once Mercury had finished with it, it was a very odd and disappointing mix of copper on a dark green background. The gatefold sleeve contained the full song lyrics in a medieval-style font, supposedly carved into two large, crumbling stone tablets, together with eight live-stage shots of the band down the outer edges of the sleeve.

Despite this inauspicious debut, Syme would design each and every album cover for the rest of the band's career. As vinyl gave way to the all-conquering CD, much of his intricate talent could get overlooked in the smaller-scale format. To counter this, Syme would incorporate many images into the incredibly detailed CD booklets, which would be a feature of Rush 4.0's output.

The cover should have been impressive; like the album it contains, it's flawed. There are no doubts as to the extent of the band's writing and performance ambitions, but overall, *Caress Of Steel* is a tougher animal to love than its predecessor. The sound is darker, and the production is less powerful. When it's good, it's very good. 'Bastille Day' is exceptional, and 'Lakeside Park' shows a highly melodic, evocative side. But sandwiched in between these two is the awkward, semi-comedic boogie of 'I Think I'm Going Bald', which is a fish out of water compared to the weightier music and lyrical themes which extend across the album's two remaining lengthier tracks.

Yet, ironically, it was the long, conceptual pieces which the fans would hold close to their hearts. If you preferred thoughtful words and long and intricate musical sections and wanted more from your music than your average band could produce, 'progressive' music was your 'go-to' genre. Rush were all that and more; eschewing the prominence of keyboards in the work of inspirational bands like Yes and Genesis, they took the ideas of 'prog' they liked and gave them a good kicking with loud guitars, busy bass and jaw-dropping drumming. Of course, Geddy's voice was, at worst, distinctive and, at best, totally original. Rush stood out. Instantly.

Fans saw and heard a band with ideas and musical 'chops' that didn't sound like anyone else. Peart's imagination and intelligence, allied with his bandmates' evolving complex compositional skills, created magical worlds, places only fans could access and enjoy. It was an intoxicating blend of multiple talents. In Vinay Menon's book *Rush – An Oral History Uncensored,* Alex explained the background to the new album:

> We wanted to work in a longer format, with more dynamics, quiet parts and loud parts. We were feeling the progressive movement of the time with Yes, Genesis, King Crimson, bands like that. We were becoming more sophisticated and complex in our arrangements, or at least trying to. We were still really young.

'Bastille Day' (4.37)

This is an absolute belter. And, like 'Anthem' before it, the opening riff does not feature again in the rest of the song. Staccato bursts of bass and drums puncture the initial riff, which just explodes into the verse theme, driven along by the energetic rhythm duo. It's just a shame that it sounds like Lifeson is playing through a cheap practice amplifier.

Lyrically, Peart is, of course, on point. Writing a rock song based around the commemoration of the storming of The Bastille in France in 1789 is a bold step, but he carries it off with style. His words are more allegorical reinterpretation than historical document and address the need for revolutionary fervour to overthrow a tyrannical form of government.

Musically, 'Bastille Day' is strong, melodic, well-constructed, and supremely effective. The chorus falls into a half-time tempo feel, allowing the subsequent repeat of the opening riff and the second verse to carry greater power. The instrumental section is concise and cleverly arranged. The first part (1.45 – 1.54) involves truncated chord stabs of the chorus progression, the second (1.54 – 2.14) has a beautifully phrased melody from Lifeson over a restrained backing from Lee and Peart, while the third (2.14 – 2.48) has the guitarist let off the leash with a more adventurous solo over a busy backing. This is inventive stuff which then moves effortlessly into the main riff, and a third verse and chorus.

The closing section of the song shows equal levels of inspiration and control. The chord-stabs section is repeated at 3.23, and then the progression which underpinned Lifeson's main solo is reprised (but this time without the solo) at 3.32. At 3.51, a new riff played in octaves is introduced, which mimics the initial riff in its climb up the fretboard but then gives way to a final, anthemic-sounding coda at 4.05. Here, the chorus melody is reprised at a slower tempo, with Lifeson providing the vocal melody with great expression and control and a second line of harmonised guitars.

This was the first Rush song I heard. I had bought *All The World's A Stage* as an experimental taster of this new band, and the live version blows its studio counterpart out of the water.

'I Think I'm Going Bald' (3.38)

Another coincidence; the second track of the 'new' band's second album is again another puzzling disappointment after such a sterling opener. Vaguely funky, slightly bluesy in places, and held together in a steady 4/4 time, the lyrics are the main issue. Perhaps intended to be light-hearted, in reality, they just sound plain odd. The song is partly a good-humoured dig at touring buddies Kiss (who had a song called 'Goin' Blind' on their 1974 album *Hotter Than Hell*) and partly Lifeson's concern regarding the effects of ageing and the possibility of hair loss. This is not something a 22-year-old should really be worrying about at that time of life!

Musically, a much heavier and more impressive riff barges in at the one-minute mark. When this section is repeated, after Lifeson's solo and a third verse, a glimmer of the band's characteristic independent determination shines through: 'My life is slipping away, I'm ageing every day, but even when I'm grey, I'll still be grey my way.'

As if to emphasise the paucity of ideas here, the last minute of the song is given over to a play-out, which goes on for far too long. Lifeson improvises away, and Peart rolls around his kit impressively, but it's all to little effect. Eventually, the track fades away, and we all hope that this has been an aberration.

'Lakeside Park' (4.07)

The third song brings another change of direction. 'Lakeside Park' has a more relaxed and melodic feel throughout. Combining this with evocative lyrics and expressive vocal work, it shows a further facet of Rush. Peart's collection of personal memories ('Midway hawkers calling 'Try your luck with me") is excellent, and the catchy chorus adds some beautiful phased electric guitar. This leads into a brief arpeggiated interlude, which culminates with a single, sustained power chord.

The band repeats the introduction and, following the second verse, Lifeson plays an excellent solo prior to the second chorus with a repeat of the interlude. The music then pivots seamlessly into a new section which contains the song's best lyrics, 'Everyone would gather on the twenty fourth of May, sitting in the sand to watch the fireworks display. Dancing fires on the beach, singing songs together, although it's just a memory, some memories last forever'. Lee's delivery of this is superb. The music gathers strength, building to a climax of descending phrases and ending with some delicate guitar harmonics.

'The Necromancer' (Total Time: 12.29)
1: Into The Darkness (0.00 – 3.47)
Some spooky-sounding reverse-recorded guitar immediately sets up an atmosphere of menace and tension. Spacious guitar chords appear and hang in the cold air. Then, eyebrows are raised for the first time; Peart's studio-manipulated delivery gives a convincing impression of the dramatic tone of voice heard introducing a trailer for a forthcoming thriller film.

> As grey traces of dawn tinge the eastern sky, the three travellers, men of Willowdale, emerge from the forest's shadow. Fording the River Dawn, they turn south, journeying into the dark and forbidding lands of the Necromancer. Even now, the intensity of his dread power can be felt, weakening the body and saddening the mind. Ultimately, they will become empty, mindless spectres, stripped of will and soul; only their thirst for freedom gives them a hunger for vengeance.

'Willowdale' and 'River Dawn' are, of course, local geographical references. Fans living south of this area must have wondered which part of the suburbs of Toronto had so displeased Peart that he had chosen such a location for this disturbing narrative.

A slow drum beat and more moody noodlings increase the unsettling feel. Lee then takes up the story from the traveller's perspective as the music subsides and tells us what we already know: 'Silence shrouds the forest as the birds announce the dawn. Three travellers ford the river and southward journey on. The road is lined with peril, the air is charged with fear, the shadow of his nearness weighs like iron tears.'

What is the point of the voiceover? And why are the trio travelling there? These issues are ignored as multiple Lifesons provide interweaving and contrasting solo lines. His work here is excellent, anguished and full of feel and phrasing over the relentlessly slow 4/4 tempo.

2: 'Under The Shadow' (3.48 – 8.37)
First up, is an important update from the desk of Neil Peart, over more threatening, atmospheric background effects: 'Shreds of black cloud loom in overcast skies. The Necromancer keeps watch with magic prism eyes. He views all his lands and is already aware of the three helpless invaders trapped in his lair.' Magic prism eyes. Available for purchase in the cinema foyer now.

An aggressive drum run treated with delay leads into the heaviest part of both this track and the album. A menacing, staccato riff, played in octaves on bass and guitar in perfect sync with the drums over a steady 4/4 time, allows Lee to paraphrase Peart's broadcast, his voice suitably angst-ridden and frustrated. The high point of this section is his delivery of the final line, 'They bow defeated.'

At 5.28, the music lurches into another instrumental section with Lifeson's guitar swooping back and forth between the left and right stereo channels, the delayed notes chasing him around the sonic space. Meanwhile, Lee and Peart are busy in their respective departments, the three coming together with a majestic unison riff at 6.33, ending with another titanic power chord. The brief reappearance of the buzzy 'By-Tor' bass sound ushers in a furious new section; energetic, angry, and intense, this extended solo section features plenty of sterling playing from all three performers. Multiple guitars vie with each other before another unison riff finally brings matters to an abrupt close.

3: Return Of The Prince' (8.38 – 12.29)
Over a very pretty arpeggiated guitar progression, we go, for one last time, over to Peart: 'Enter the champion, Prince By-Tor appears. To battle for freedom from chains of long years. The spell has been broken, the dark clouds are bright, and the wraith of the Necromancer soars away out of sight.'

The final section has an appropriately uplifting and positive feel; major key chords and a bright texture throughout lighten the tale. Far be it from me to nit-pick on character details, but Prince By-Tor is now a good guy? Just an album ago, he batted for the other team, in a manner of speaking.

This inconsistency aside, the rest of the track is a satisfying cruise through a sunny musical landscape, with a distorted guitar adding an excellent, understated and supremely effective solo, the music going into the fade.

Overall, 'The Necromancer' is an intriguing and, at times, very impressive piece of work. Following on from 'By-Tor', Rush take the musical bull by the horns and, with the second side of the album, really unleash the horses. Follow me for more mixed metaphors!

'The Fountain Of Lamneth' (Total Time: 19.58)
In the *Classic Rock* interview, Alex admitted:

> *Caress Of Steel* was very ambitious.'The Fountain Of Lamneth' was a story about life, which was a little precocious of us, three guys in their early 20s.

> When we made that record, we were still a very young band, learning our skills. We'd only been touring a year when we made that record. It was our jumping-off point.

This epic piece is nowhere near as indulgent as some critics make out when approached as a selection of varied, melodic rock songs of different hues. In the main, it's interesting and, at times, compelling. Luckily, the entire tale is written in the first person, thereby denying the listener the pleasure of any more Peart monologues.

In an interview with *Sounds* magazine in 1977, Peart explained his inspiration for the track. On a cruise on a mountainside road, he stopped at a cliff edge and observed the city lights beneath him:

> I got to thinking: what would life be like if you could only measure your position as a person by the level at which you lived up the side of a mountain?

The composition could also be interpreted as an allegory for Peart's life thus far, leaving his comfortable upbringing and lifestyle, journeying across the ocean to find artistic fulfilment in another land, only to encounter disappointment. However, this setback did not diminish his desire to achieve success.

I: 'In The Valley' (0.00 – 4.13)

A song of two sections (which are neatly reprised for the finale 'The Fountain',) 'In The Valley' opens with some delicately picked 12-string acoustic guitar arpeggios as Lee sets the scene: 'I am born, I am me, I am new, I am free. Look at me, I am young, sight unseeing, life unsung.' His soft voice is superb here, elegantly supported by just enough reverberation.

At 1.02, Lifeson introduces a rising progression of vigorously strummed chords. This is then matched by the full rock trio instrumentation, replicating the progression with accuracy and aggression, replete with some superb drum fills. This new theme moves into a new, heavier chord sequence, gathers intensity and leads into the verse describing the protagonist's young life: 'My eyes have just been opened and they're open very wide. Images around me don't identify inside. Just one blur I recognize, the one that soothes and feeds. My way of life is easy, and as simple are my needs.

The music then relaxes into a gentler section: 'Yet my eyes are drawn towards the mountain in the east. Fascinates and captivates, gives my heart no peace. The mountain holds the sunrise in the bosom of the night till bursting forth from rocky chains, the valley floods with light.'

Then it's back to the noise and anguish, where Lee concludes that he 'lives to climb that mountain to the Fountain of Lamneth.' The relaxed section appears again with the same lyrics as before. The *sturm und drang* returns and builds to a hectic, dramatic conclusion…

II: 'Didacts And Narpets' (4.17 – 5.16)

Avant-garde, bordering on ridiculous, and the shortest composition to appear on any Rush album, this track, fabulous drumming aside, is about as enjoyable as standing on an upturned electric plug with your bare feet.

The lyrics, such as they are, won't win any awards. An intense tirade against teachers (didacts) and 'narpets' (an anagram of parents) is just embarrassing. Dramatic power chords punctuate the aggressive drum solo accompanied by 'Stay. Go. Work. No. Earn. Live. Earn. Give. Stay or fight. What's right?' This all builds to a terrific crescendo of thunderous drums, distorted guitars, and Geddy in full angst mode, finishing things off with a climactic shout of 'Listen!'

To which the obvious answer is, 'No, thanks', and move swiftly on to the next track. No doubt, an attempt at reflecting the anger, confusion, and energy of teenage years, the absence of 'Didacts And Narpets' would strengthen the flow of 'The Fountain Of Lamneth'.

III: 'No One At The Bridge' (5.20 – 9.36)

So, in between the valley and the mountain, there has to be an ocean? This must be the case; otherwise, why am I hearing waves? The maritime mood is emphasised by a rolling 6/8 time signature and a relaxing chord arpeggio pattern. Clearly, there has been some sort of problem on board, as Lee advises us in full rock voice mode: 'Writhing back to consciousness, the coldness grips my skin, the sky is pitching violently, drawn by shrieking winds. Sea spray blurs my vision, the waves roll by so fast, save my ship for freedom, I'm lashed helpless to the mast.' A more restrained approach here would sound better, allowing Lee to give full rein to his vocals in the chorus. Here, he sounds like he's overdoing it.

Another verse usefully recalls the early days of the journey and reveals that the narrator's crew deserted him just when he needed help. At 2.16, the superb chorus cuts in dramatically, with staccato chords and a heavy, rocking rhythm. The vocals here are magnificent and, allied to the powerfully abrupt accompaniment, provide a genuine highpoint in the song. The music quietens again, with Lifeson adding a superb, maturely melodic solo reminiscent of Steve Hackett's work with Genesis. This builds to a zenith over the verse chord progression. The solo sounds proud and confident, and the mood is suddenly lifted as the song fades away on a single chord to the sound of some (uncredited) seagulls and the ocean.

IV: 'Panacea' (9.38 – 12.52)

Time must have passed in the telling of this tale because now, for some reason, we go all Renaissance style classical guitar in this attractive piece, which has echoes of 'Rivendell'. The narrator has found a place of solace and fallen in love, but this is not enough to quell his ambition.

Lee is back to his soft voice for this peaceful interlude. Some very pretty, clean electric picking is added for the 'I catch the smell of ambergris' section, and bass and drums join in for the relaxed chorus to this gentle ballad. A repeat of the introduction and a second verse, this time featuring the addition of some effective, violined guitars, emphasises the sense of peace and meaning the narrator feels in this place. But even this is not enough for him and the second chorus signals the end of his time in this paradise: 'My heart will lie beside you and my wandering body grieves.'

V: 'Bacchus Plateau' (12.53 – 16.07)
The mood changes abruptly again, with some faded in major key chords and the bass and drums soon adding to the positive musical feel.

Despite its up-tempo, uplifting music, the lyrical mood has swung downward, especially in the second verse: 'Another foggy dawn, the mountain almost gone. Another doubtful fear, the road is not so clear. My soul grows ever weary and the end is ever near.' The catchy chorus is outstanding: 'Draw another goblet from the cask of '43. Crimson misty memory, hazy glimpse of me. Give me back my wonder, I've something more to give. I guess it doesn't matter, there's not much more to, not much more to live.' It's great to hear Peart dispense with any clever rhythmic colouring here, he just goes full four-to-the-floor rock drummer here, to excellent effect.

A final chorus is followed by a short Lifeson solo, which fades away into the left stereo channel as the chords of the finale crash into...

VI: 'The Fountain' (16.08 – 19.58)
The hopeful narrator has arrived at his destination, but disappointment soon sets in: 'Now at last I fall before the Fountain of Lamneth. I thought I would be singing but I'm tired, out of breath. Many journeys end here, but the secret's still the same. Life is just a candle and a dream must give it flame.'

The angst returns with a vengeance, but the singer remains resolute despite his disappointment: 'Like old sol behind the mountain, I'll be coming up again.' A return to the more peaceful section and a soulful solo from Lifeson impresses yet again with his phrasing and feel. A hurried, heavy power chord build-up brings the track to what sounds like a conclusion, but the opening 12-string acoustic pattern is re-established with soft vocals finally bringing the tale to an end: 'I'm in motion, I am still, I am crying, I am still, I'm together, I'm apart, I'm forever, at the start. Still – I am.'

The final guitar chord is followed by a gentle swell chord of guitar, bass, and cymbals and it's all over. Ambitious, creative, and, at times, hugely impressive, neither 'The Fountain Of Lamneth' nor the rest of the album would set the rock world alight. In an interview with *The Boston Globe* in 1990, Peart was less than enthusiastic about *Caress Of Steel*, saying:

> When I look back at that stuff now, I see the flaws very apparently, the disjointedness of a lot of it. If your mother drags out your grade two

crayon drawings, you're obviously not going to look at them as the pinnacle of your life.

In *Contents Under Pressure,* Geddy felt that:

'Fountain of Lamneth' was just something we had to do. We were a young band, a little pretentious, full of ambitions, full of grand ideas, and we wanted to see if we could make some of those grand ideas happen. And 'Fountain of Lamneth' was the first attempt at that. And I think there are some beautiful moments, but a lot of it is ponderous and off the mark.

In the same book, Alex summarised the album:

That was a very experimental album for us. On *Fly By Night,* we had 'By-Tor'. 'So that was the precursor to this. 'Necromancer' was an extension of 'By-Tor'. But 'The Fountain Of Lamneth' became even more of that experimental, full-side, thematic ... I don't want to say opera, but concept kind of record. We were experimenting then to see what would work. It was really important for us to do that. The record company hated it. It was the least commercially successful record that we've done.

Ambitious, multi-layered, complex and yet still largely accessible, *Caress Of Steel* was, despite its critical and commercial disappointments, essential for what Rush would record next. Without *Caress Of Steel*, there wouldn't have been, in all likelihood, *2112*.

2112

Personnel:
Alex Lifeson: guitars
Geddy Lee: bass guitar, vocals
Neil Peart: drums, percussion
Hugh Syme: synthesizer ('2112') and Mellotron ('Tears')
Recorded at Toronto Sound Studios, Toronto
Produced by Rush and Terry Brown
Released: 1 April 1976 on Mercury Records
All music composed by Lee & Lifeson with lyrics by Peart, except 'Changes' (Lifeson) and 'Tears' (Lee)
Chart positions: Canada: 5, US: 61, UK: did not chart

If it wasn't for *2112*, Rush would probably have ended up as an interesting but obscure footnote in the history of Canadian rock. As things turned out, the album, the first of what many fans believe to be the start of a Golden Era for the band, secured their future.

In his 2006 book *Roadshow – Landscape With Drums – A Concert Tour By Motorcycle*, Peart wrote:

> The band's first album had been recorded just before I joined, and when it sold 125,000 copies in the United States, the record company pronounced it 'a promising debut'. When the next one, *Fly By Night,* sold 125,000 copies, it was 'a solid follow up.' But when the third album, *Caress Of Steel,* sold 125,000 copies, they called it 'a dog' We were urged to be 'more commercial' and write some 'singles'. So, in our contrarian fashion, we recorded an ambitious and impassioned sidelong piece about a future dystopia, along with a few other weird songs, and released our fourth album, *2112,* early in 1976. It was considered by the bean counters to be our last chance, and without any promotion from them, it was something of a snowball's chance.

Rush toured to promote *Caress Of Steel*, this time as support to Kiss and Mott The Hoople. However, when they headlined their own gigs, audience numbers were down. The density and complexity of the new album puzzled radio stations. A lack of airplay meant a low turnout of new fans, and so the venues became smaller. It was with no little irony that this excursion was dubbed the 'Down The Tubes' tour. Following a break for Christmas, the tour finally wound up back at the Massey Hall, Toronto, in January 1976.

While other bands might have grown despondent, Rush got annoyed. They refused to bow to the demands of their record label and were determined to make the music they wanted to make. It was a brave strategy. Interestingly, export sales were increasing around the world, with particular interest coming from Europe and Japan. Readers of *Circus* magazine voted Rush the second-best new group of the year, so clearly, the rewards were out there;

they were just widely and unevenly distributed. As far as Rush was concerned, if they were going to get burnt by the record business, the fire would be one of their own making. They resolved to make a better album than *Caress Of Steel*, one that was more aggressive, heavier, and direct. In *Contents Under Pressure,* Geddy recalled:

> '2112' is probably the most important thing we've ever written. Without that song, we would not have continued as a band. It was largely written in the studio and in rehearsal, and I think we had four weeks to make that record, so we got an extra week out of the deal from *Caress Of Steel*. And it just came together. Even some of the heavier parts Alex and I wrote just sitting down together with acoustic guitars. The concept came together very clearly and very quickly. We just had these riffs we wanted to put together, and it just started to click for that song. And that whole album is very much like that.

The basic ideas which underpinned '2112' began with some lyrics, again inspired by Ayn Rand's novel *Anthem*. Peart saw an obvious parallel between her main characters' striving for independence in the face of a totalitarian regime and the band's own predicament. Rand was seen by Rush as an artistic figurehead to admire, not a political philosophy to follow. Certain sections of the music media did not dig as deeply, and lazy criticism of right-wing bias was regularly thrown at the band.

2112 benefits from a greater focus than the sprawling ideas which had featured on the lengthier tracks on *Caress Of Steel*. This clarity of purpose translated into the now iconic album sleeve design; a naked man, alluding to the classical nude depiction of purity, faces the red pentagram of the Federation. The inner sleeves of the gatefold design featured the lyrics, also red on a black background, while the back sleeve had the legendary 'kimono' shot of the trio, with Lifeson's trousers being so tight that you could tell which religion he followed. When the album was presented to Mercury, the record company's enthusiasm did not match that of its creators. Art imitated life; the business priests were dismissive of what was brought before them by the young artists, eager to share their creation with the world.

2112 was a gamble for all concerned. Rush had to deliver, both musically and financially. That the album is still held up today as the first of the band's masterpieces is a testament to their vision, resilience, and resolve to do things on their own terms. A Randian approach, for sure, but one that celebrates the benefits of ambition and independence. *2112* simultaneously saved and made Rush. Mercury benefited hugely from Lee, Lifeson, and Peart's dogged persistence to do what they wanted and to hell with the consequences.

Within three months of its release, *2112* had sold over 160,000 copies. Another first for the band was that the costs of recording were recouped by sales of the album alone. *2112* became an 'underground' album. Word of mouth, arguably the most effective form of advertising ever devised, grew. And grew. And grew. Heavier than *Caress Of Steel* and yet still layered, *2112* was more relatable and accessible, whether at home in front of the stereo speakers or at a venue facing the full might of the band's PA system.

In a neat reversal of the track listing on *Caress Of Steel* (three shorter songs, a mini-epic of three songs, and then the entire second side dedicated to the six-song strong epic), *2112* hit its listeners straight away with the ground-breaking suite of seven songs that comprised the title track. Side two, as this was in the days of vinyl and cassette, presented five shorter songs of differing hues and moods. In the *Classic Rock* interview, Geddy recalled:

> We finished the tour and went straight in and made this record. Nobody at Mercury knew what we were doing. There was no playing of demos for the label or our manager. I've never done that in my whole life. From day one, we never had anyone in the control room with us, other than our producer Terry Brown. Before we got in the studio, we had the layout of the album already planned: the big piece on side one and the shorter songs on side two. Having those shorter songs is a nice break from the heavy concept of side one. And we had 'Something For Nothing' to end the album, because the sentiment in that song related back to the story of '2112' in some sort of abstract sense.

Aware that fans may be a bit baffled by the complexities of hearing the title track to their new album for the first time at concerts, the band produced the following flyer, which was handed out at the venues:

> In the year 2062, a galaxy-wide war results in the union of all the planets under the rule of the Red Star of the Solar Federation. The world is controlled by computers, called 'Temples', which determine all reading matter, songs, pictures…everything connected with life during the year 2112 ('The Temples Of Syrinx').
>
> In the midst of all this assembly line living, a man discovers what was once known years before as a guitar ('Discovery'). The man begins to pluck the strings and turn the knobs, discovering that he can make his own music – music much different than that of the Temples. He rushes to tell the priests of his discovery ('Presentation'), but to the man's dismay, the priests dismiss the instrument, saying it doesn't fit the plan of the Solar Federation.
>
> The man returns to the cave in which he found the guitar and, during a dream, is led by an oracle to a land of incredible beauty and serenity ('Oracle: A Dream'). Upon awakening, he cannot believe it was a dream – the beauty was so real.
>
> He remains in the cave for several days, becoming more and more depressed with each passing hour ('Soliloquy'). The man decides he can not go on as part of the Federation and takes his life to move on to a better one.

As he dies, another planetary battle begins ('Grand Finale'), with the outcome to be determined in the mind of the listener.

'2112' (20.39)
The scene was set on the rear of the original gatefold sleeve with the following text, signed 'Anonymous' and dated '2112'.

> I lie awake, staring out at the bleakness of Megadon. City and sky become one, merging into a single plane, a vast sea of unbroken grey. The Twin Moons just two pale orbs as they trace their way across the steely sky. I used to think I had a pretty good life here, just plugging into my machine for the day, then watching Templevision or reading a Temple paper in the evening.
>
> My friend Jon always told me it was nicer here than under the atmospheric domes of the Outer Planets. We have had peace since 2062, when the surviving planets were banded together under the Red Star of the Solar Federation. The less fortunate gave us a few moons.
>
> I believed what I was told, I thought it was a good life, I thought I was happy. Then I found something which changed it all ...

I: 'Overture' (0.00 – 4.33)
The band's first instrumental track (discounting the Biblical quotation right at the close of the piece) is an absolute stormer! This piece, the last to be written for the overall composition, is the sound of a band going down in flames while drinking heavily on a cocktail of mixed metaphors at the last chance saloon. They have never sounded better in their four-album career.

Rush, never ones to do things by halves, take the classical music idea of an overture as a piece designed to get an audience's attention and proceed to hit their listeners straight between the ears, laying out the musical landscape that is to come. As a statement of intent, 'Overture' perfectly encapsulates what '2112' is all about – loud, aggressive, precise and, above all, wondrously exciting music.

The track, moment by moment:

0.00 – 0.47: Syme's ghostly, unsettling, multi-tracked ARP Odyssey synthesizer creates the dystopian future mood while, in the background, repeated pairs of heavy bass notes suggest large-scale industrial activity, some sort of surveillance or possibly a heartbeat. In *Classic Albums – 2112 And Moving Pictures,* Geddy said:

> Hugh Syme, who does our album covers, was in the sessions. He had played Mellotron on the song 'Tears', and he had this little ARP and we just recorded a whole lot of him just playing around with the APR, making space sounds. We knew we wanted to start the song with a kind of sound that had the

> imagery of soaring through space, moving through time. Afterwards, we just listened back to all the bits that he had played and we picked one that was the best, so it was kind of a one-off combination of improvisation and playing with buttons and knobs. I assume he knew what he was doing, but I think it was a little bit of luck involved.

Given his involvement in the now iconic synthesiser introduction, Syme should really have been given a composer's credit and subsequent royalties.
0.48 – 1.18: The introduction to 'The Temples Of Syrinx' is heard as the synthesizer vanishes. The chords are played staccato, with some excellent delay and stereo panning being introduced when the theme is repeated.
1.19 – 1.32: A fanfare, an excerpt from 'Oracle: The Dream', briefly appears before a sustained power chord drives us headlong into…
1.33 – 1.59: The chord progression from the chorus of 'The Temples Of Syrinx' with Lee's otherworldly voice rising through the octaves in the background. The music climaxes, changing into …
2.00 – 2.32: A new chord-based section similar to the quieter sections of 'Presentation' with an uplifting, major key feel. Two electric guitars support some excellent drum fills and bass lines.
2.33 – 2.45: The chord sequence from 'The Temples Of Syrinx' is heard again, this time as a series of single sustained power chords with more drum and bass fills.
2.46 – 3.05: A furious, twisting guitar riff from Lifeson is punctuated by powerful stabs from Lee and Peart, followed by a descending chord sequence which lessens the tension slightly before …
3.06 – 3.34: Over a 'half-tempo' rhythmic feel, Lifeson plays a glorious solo, wrenching all manner of pain from his guitar.
3.36 – 4.07: A busier section with an up-tempo, almost funky feel as electric and acoustic guitars, bass, and drums all fill the sonic space.
4.08 – 4.25: Another angst-filled guitar line, a humorous homage to the coda section of Pytor Tchaikovsky's 1882 composition, '1812 Overture', is dominant above all the power of the rhythm section; it's fast and passionate, culminating in a short reprise of part of 'The Temples of Syrinx' chords before repeated power chords and thunderous explosions usher in the end of the instrumental music.
4.26 – 4.33: The briefest of quiet interludes where a close-miked Lee sings, 'And the meek shall inherit the earth' over Lifeson's subtle guitar arpeggios. It's the calm before the storm …

II: 'The Temples Of Syrinx' (4.34 – 6.45)

No other track captures the frustration and determination of Rush at this point in their career as this one. Furious and passionate, and one of the first songs to be written for the album, all three players pound their instruments to their limits. This metallic assault scythes through the speakers with a relentless power which still impresses 40 years on.

'The Temples Of Syrinx' is the band's heaviest track to date and is not that far removed from the fury and bile that much of the coming punk rock storm would revel in. Fast, aggressive, and committed throughout, it is Lee's vocal performance that astonishes the most. Another asset is the track's brevity: an introduction, a verse and chorus and repeat and it's all over in just over two minutes, rounded off in an unexpected fashion with a brief, beautiful coda on the classical guitar.

In the band's later years, it would be 'Overture' and 'The Temples Of Syrinx', which would mainly be performed under the banner of '2112'. On occasion, 'Grand Finale' would also be added, but it was not until 1997's *Different Stages – Live* triple album that the composition would be played in its entirety. Given that this was two decades later than the original recording, the band detuned their instruments by two semitones to accommodate the effects of time and touring on Lee's voice. This decision also made '2112' even heavier and more satisfying.

III: 'Discovery' (6.46 – 9.46)

Our hero discovers a long abandoned electric guitar in a cave with a waterfall, the sound of falling water courtesy of a sound effects record. He slowly brings it into standard tuning (how does he know how to do this?) and then begins to play. Through a working amplifier. Close to a water source. Seriously? Well, this *is* science fiction, so I guess 'anything can happen'.

Back in reality, 'Discovery' was played on a 'clean' sounding Fender Stratocaster, which Alex had borrowed from a friend. It was recorded in real-time; what we hear is what happened in the studio, with no editing or overdubs.

A steel-strung acoustic guitar would have been a better choice here, being more representative of the themes of individuality and freedom of expression. Such a change would also make the sonic contrasts in 'Presentation' more effective. Again, I recommend the *Different Stages* performance of '2112' a listen; Lifeson's version of this song 20 years on is superb, beautiful and inventive.

The guitarist gives a convincing impression of the situation the narrator finds himself in, soon constructing a pretty little instrumental, replete with tasteful use of natural harmonics. It is interesting that none of the three themes heard here are present in 'Overture', reinforcing the idea that the narrator is finding something new and unusual. Lee's gentle vocals bring the scene to life. An accelerating and uplifting new chord sequence becomes brightly enthusiastic ('See how it sings…'). This slows and calms into a drone-based melody section, which changes into a relaxed progression, becoming …

IV: 'Presentation' (9.47 – 13.58)

… a new scene where the narrator approaches the Priests with his discovery. His voice is characterised by the soft music of 'Discovery', whereas the Priests are 'metal personified'. A sonic blast of power chords, heavy bass and drums signifies their appearance. The music reverts to a quieter section ('I know it's most unusual to come before you so ...') before the furious response is unleashed ('Yes, we know, it's nothing new ...'). Another change of dynamics signals the narrator's disbelief at their reaction, with the argument going back and forth with a noisy 'Don't annoy us further ...' exchange.

An instrumental based around the chorus chord progression of 'The Temples of Syrinx' follows, with Lifeson throwing everything he's got into his solo, including spectacular wah-wah pedal abuse, some rapid flurries of notes and a suitably anguished tone. The music comes to a sudden ending on a sustained chord of D major.

V: 'Oracle: The Dream' (13.59 – 15.59)

Maintaining the D major tonality, this is another change of place and pace with a deeply atmospheric, slow chord sequence, drenched in reverb reflecting the narrator's dismay at the rejection ('I wandered home through silent streets ...') sung with a soft voice. An upward spiralling sound effect changes the mood completely into a superbly metallic main section.

Falling asleep, he is transported into a dream of his planet's history, an ancient, freer world constructed by 'The Elders', a time which, after the Priests have fallen from power, will come again. This is driven along by a magnificently heavy chord sequence which is strident and proud in its delivery. The chorus section features a chord sequence from 'Overture'.

The final section of lyrics ('They left our planets long ago, the elder race still learn and grow. Their power grows with purpose strong to claim the home where they belong. Home to tear the Temples down, home to change') sets up the events which appear in 'Grand Finale'.

VI: 'Soliloquy' (16.00 – 18.20)

We are back in the 'waterfall cave' and another delicate, clean-sounding chord progression. The narrator's mood is one of deep despair, again using the sonic contrasts of quiet passages and savage distortion to describe his depressed state. The beautiful mix of 'clean' guitar, vocal melody and reverb is destroyed by a heavy sequence with guitar, bass, drums and vocals again reaching their peak of expression.

Lifeson's solo after Lee's desperate concluding line 'My lifeblood spills over' is masterful, full of pain, passion and precision. Inspired by his dream, the narrator's suicide presents a very 'Stoical' response to oppression, allowing his mind to travel to a different realm.

VII: 'Grand Finale' (18.21 – 20.39)

Another instrumental, originally called 'Denouement', closes the track, but this one, while still relentless, has a more optimistic feel due to its greater use of major chords. Its chugging nature and driving rhythm suggest a hoped-for, positive future.

A heavy descending chord progression heralds in a fast and furious section, again with Lifeson's wah-wah pedal getting a *lot* of abuse as the music then rises and builds to the dramatic conclusion and the voiceover. The final words, narrated by Peart, are of unknown origin ('Attention all planets of the Federation, we have assumed control') and are open to interpretation. Who is this 'we'?

In the *Classic Rock* interview, Geddy admitted:

> The ending of that story was purposefully ambiguous. What happens in that ending is either liberation or the invasion of another totalitarian state. It's for the listener to decide which, based on their own sense of life.

If only this tale had been carried onto the second side of the album with a definitive conclusion. But Rush wanted to make us think rather than provide simple solutions to the situation they had set up. I would have quite happily sat through another 20 minutes of this epic tale, treating the gap where the record is flipped over as a short interval in the band's intensely involving space opera. Fans would have to wait until 2012 for Rush to actually release their only full concept album, 'Clockwork Angels'. As it stands, side two is a very different musical animal.

'A Passage To Bangkok' (3.35)

Opening with a suitably intense guitar riff, to which some 'oriental' harmonies are briefly added, 'A Passage To Bangkok' (Peart's tip of the cap to E.M.Forster's 1924 novel *A Passage To India*) is a curious amalgam of heavy rock, tongue-in-cheek humour, and catchy commerciality.

Compared to much of *2112*, this song has an upbeat feel within its driving rhythmic structure, appealing chorus, and a vague whiff of Led Zeppelin's 'Kashmir' as an influence. There's plenty of hard rock to enjoy here as well, and some clever moments: Peart shifting his drum rhythm to a syncopated two and four-beat basis during the instrumental section, the harmony guitar lines in the verses and Lee's exuberant vocal delivery of the evocative lyrics.

Lifeson's solo is suitably gritty for the instrumental section, which brings about a brief reprise of the 'Oriental' harmony and a repeat of the choruses to bring this enjoyable track to a positive close.

'A Passage To Bangkok' is fun, melodic, powerful, inventive and a tacit acknowledgement of the chemical assistance the band indulged in during the early stages of their recording career. It would make appearances on subsequent live albums, starting with a surprise inclusion on *Exit Stage Left*, and is the second-best song on the second side of the record.

'The Twilight Zone' (3.19)

This song was a last-minute composition required to get the album's running time up to an acceptable level. It is also one of producer Terry Brown's preferred tracks. In an interview with *Prog* magazine in January 2015, he said:

> 'The Twilight Zone' is a little gem with a very strong lead guitar motif from Alex. Ged's verse vocals are up in the stratosphere and then the chorus slips into an eerie flanged vocal that is in the 'zone'. This is all held together by Neil's very concise, driving percussion closing with the airy guitar solo, which makes this one of my favourite Rush tunes.

The track is a musical imagining of an episode from the landmark Sci-Fi television series of the same name made by Rod Serling (1924 – 1975), to whom *Caress Of Steel* had been dedicated. And, like the show itself, this is the strangest track on the album; at times light-hearted, at others heavily atmospheric and tense.

There are hints of Thin Lizzy's harmonised twin guitar attack in the introduction, and the second chorus features Lee both whispering and singing the words, which is unsettling, especially when listening through headphones. After the second chorus, Lifeson has a spacious, tortured solo, which makes much use of the space in between his phrases as the song comes to an end.

'Lessons' (3.53)

The opening recalls 'Making Memories' with its briskly strummed, major key, acoustic guitar introduction, relaxed bass and drum contributions. The chorus is a muscular affair of crashing power chords, aggressive drums, and a very active bassist thrashing out an excellent contrasting section of music.

The track quietens for the second verse while maintaining its pace and energy already established. Another heavy chorus leads into a fabulous, grinding chord groove, with Lifeson again giving his all, which continues as the mood switches back to the acoustic blend. This turns into a playout with the guitarist clearly enjoying himself as the song powers along into the fade.

'Tears' (3.34)

In his book *The Art Of Rush,* Hugh Syme recalled:

> 'Tears' was a beautiful song written by Geddy. It was one of the more exposed and emotional songs. When I heard it I thought, 'There's an awful lot of room to work with here' So I went down the hall for two hours and worked up some Mellotron parts and some ARP synthesizer horn parts. I also did some strings and flute overdubs on Mellotron and the French horn sound that happens in the middle of the song. It was a fun bonding time for Geddy and me. It was also the first time I'd met the band.

Sadly, this promising, understated ballad soon becomes swamped by Syme's contributions, which turns this earnest, if somewhat mawkish, composition into a syrupy mush. No doubt the original version of the song did have 'an awful lot of room to work with'; that doesn't mean that all of the available space should be filled. But it is, and it's to the song's detriment. The delicate introduction is pretty, and Lee sings his composition with sincerity, but by the time the chorus arrives, the Mellotron has assumed control of the mix, which spoils the overall effect.

Less would have been so much more here; simple guitars, sparse bass and gentle drums are all that's needed to support the vocals, although an elegant piano could have been added to great effect. However, by the end, the music is suffocated by the keyboards, and what could have been a moving island of regretful tranquillity becomes sweet and sickly to the ears.

'Something For Nothing' (4.02)

'Something For Nothing', whilst being separate and distinct from '2112' (the track), is a neat conclusion for the themes explored on side one of the album. The fact that all three members of Rush inherited a strong work ethic from their respective families informs this song and, of course, by extension, their entire career. In *Classic Albums – 2112 And Moving Pictures,* Neil said:

> It was in downtown LA, I remember. We were going through a rough part of town and spray painted on the wall was 'Freedom isn't Free'. It's common graffiti now, but it wasn't then; it was 'Whoh!' it struck me like that. So the genesis of the song was that graffiti, which I thought was kind of cool. The rest of it was more about self-actualisation, I think … it won't come to you. I think I was starting to see among my generation of people growing up there was a sense of being aggressive or passive, in the sense of 'I'm just waiting to get discovered'. Well, guys like my bandmates and I were out there getting discovered or working towards it, at least.

The closing number of the album is the track where Rush re-exert their aggressive energies and provides an anthem which, more than any other of their songs to date, exemplifies their approach to their craft. The words are straightforward, and the music is the same. The message to the listener is that the power and responsibility for improving their lives lies with themselves and no one else. It's another declaration of independence.

The song veers between pretty arpeggiated passages and driving rock sections with some monumental power-chord stabs, all of which build to a sensational chorus ('You don't get something for nothing, you don't get freedom for free, you won't get wise with the sleep still in your eyes, whatever your dream might be.') It's a manifesto for the band, and a message for their growing legions of fans, which still stands as an impressive mantra to the importance of self-reliance and determination.

'Something For Nothing' rocks along magnificently with energy and attack. Lee's voice is at times at the outer limits of his range, but he sings with a compelling conviction, especially when he gathers his strength for the coda chorus with an impressive rising 'Whoh!' (3.14). A furious play-out follows with the band really going for it as the music fades away. It's the best track on side two and is a worthy end to such a landmark recording.

In *Chemistry,* the 2005 book by Jon Collins, Alex viewed the album thus:

> We came back punching; that album still feels like that to me when I listen to it today – I can feel the hostility hanging out.

Similarly, Geddy thought:

> *2112* was the album on which the sound of Rush was born. We realised for the first time that we'd won a hard-fought battle for our independence and created a sound that was all our own.

And this is key to the success of *2112* and Rush as a band. Whereas *Rush* is the outlier of the quartet of albums released thus far, and *Fly By Night* is the debut for Rush 2.0, the band allowed their desire to ape elements of Yes and Genesis to dominate parts of *Caress Of Steel*. For instance, every time I hear the solo in 'No One At The Bridge', I always picture Steve Hackett, not Alex Lifeson, at work.

With *2112*, Rush managed to throw off such blatant vestiges and carve a place for themselves in the rock world. From this point on, they didn't sound like anybody else; they became themselves, and, in that sense, this record is the true debut of the band. The previous trio of albums can be viewed as stepping stones; some very worthy efforts are to be heard in the three discs. But it is here that Rush become Rush. And their fans, and the 'fans-to-be' were very impressed. For those of us who loved hard rock but also appreciated subtlety, intelligence, 'chops' and a distinctive sound, this was the band to watch from now on.

All The World's A Stage

Personnel:
Alex Lifeson: guitars
Geddy Lee: bass guitar, vocals
Neil Peart: drums, percussion
Recorded at Massey Hall, Toronto, by the Fedco Mobile Unit
Produced by Rush and Terry Brown
Engineered by Terry Brown
Mixed at Toronto Sound Studios, Toronto, Canada
Tape Operator: Ken Morris
Released: 29 September 1976 on Mercury Records
Chart positions: Canada: 5, US: 61, UK: did not chart

In the *Classic Rock* interview, Geddy remembered the period immediately after the release and success of the band's most important album of the 1970s:

> It was just a fantastic time. Pretty much everything changed for us with *2112*. There were a lot of growing pains in terms of what kind of live act we were becoming because we had to learn how to be a headliner and start developing a show, which we didn't really have. We had to think about providing a show and giving the people their money's worth. We were the band they were actually paying to see!

The 1970s was the decade of the double-live album. Fans wanted more than the typical 40-minute fare of studio recordings and the chance to experience the sound of a live concert was compelling. Record companies, only too keen for their next dollar, were happy to comply, and it was seen as a badge of honour to be big enough to warrant the issue of such an album. With *All The World's A Stage*, Rush joined this 'Hall Of Fame', a landscape which included, or would include, the likes of Deep Purple, Status Quo, Queen, Led Zeppelin, UFO and Thin Lizzy, amongst many others.

The famous speech in William Shakespeare's *As You Like It* provides the title for this, the first of the band's 11 live albums. Known as 'The Seven Ages Of Man', it begins with the phrase 'All the world's a stage, and all the men and women merely players'. These words would be further reinterpreted for some of the fourth verse lyrics of 'Limelight' (*Moving Pictures*): 'All the world's indeed a stage, we are merely players'.

The tour to promote *2112* resulted in the recordings, which became *All The World's A Stage*. The gigging started in February in Ontario and then moved across the United States. Despite the critics still being largely against the three Canadians' brand of progressive metal, and with Lee's voice remaining a polarising factor, the band had a fan base, a growing group of people who found their own anthem in *2112*, an album whose themes spoke to their own nature and attitude of mind.

The cover, again designed by Hugh Syme, was another stylish affair. The triple gatefold sleeve shows a stage with monitors, mic stands, drum kit, amplifiers, and lights all set for the band to deliver the goods. The naked man imagery of *2112* is superimposed between the drum kit and the overhead lights. The inner gatefold had numerous colour and black and white photos of the trio in action all shown in a variety of different lighting scenarios. The back cover had a single larger shot of the band in a high energy, possibly end-of-song power chord smash, next to the essential song list information. All of this is overlaid on a tasteful backdrop sunburst effect of blue turning to gold.

Terry Brown's recollection of this period, quoted in Martin Popoff's book' *Anthem – Rush In The '70s,* was:

> From a creative standpoint, obviously, the tunes had already been established; the arrangements and pre-production and everything, and they didn't really change a whole lot on the live record. But we had to get that magic performance and all the little details straight. Both the live records we did, quite often fans say to me. 'It's the first record I ever bought, and that's how I learned about the band'.

This is certainly true of this writer. While *All The World's A Stage* wasn't the first rock album I bought, it was my first Rush record, and it served as a perfect introduction to what this rising and yet still mysterious band were all about. Certainly, this live recording inspired me to get hold of their back catalogue and the preceding four studio albums were purchased as soon as the weekend job money savings would allow. As a consequence, I waited with breath bated for what they would do next. In essence, how do you follow *2112*? The answer, Rush being Rush, of course, was to 'expect the unexpected'.

All The World's A Stage is really 'the story so far' for the band. Three consecutive nights (11 to 13 June) were recorded at the Massey Hall in Toronto, with the majority of the material being taken from the final performance. Featuring four songs (that's three too many) from the debut, three from 'Fly By Night', only two from 'Caress Of Steel', most of the first side of '2112', plus one other song from that album; it gave potential fans an impressive window on what the band were all about. To ensure Rush was presented in the best sonic light, a month was spent mixing the album, far longer than on any previous release. The sense that the band were about to embark on something even more spectacular than what they had achieved so far was summed up in the following album notes:

> This album consists of the show that we brought to you during our North American tour of 1976. It is an anthology of what we feel to be the high points of our concerts and recordings up to this time. It is not perfect, but it is faithful to us and to you. We have tried to strike a careful balance between

> perfection and authenticity and to create a finished work that you may enjoy and we may be proud of. This album to us signifies the end of the beginning, a milestone to mark the close of chapter one, in the annals of Rush.

While all the songs on *All The World's A Stage* have already been reviewed, I thought it appropriate to bring out facets of the live performances which bear further examination and comment, especially with regard to the four songs from the debut album, which gain fresh impetus and invention from Peart's drum skills.

In an interview in 1976 quoted on the band's official website *Rush.com,* Neil said:

> When we play live, we add all our little quirks to it. It grows and our older material shows a remarkable progression. Some of the old songs have developed until they are superior to the originals. This gives us a chance to bring them up to date. We always felt there was something happening live that didn't come across on record. Now, we have the opportunity to capture the essence of the band.

'Bastille Day' (4.58)

There's a very quick fade in of crowd cheers, the voice of bass guitar roadie Skip Gildersleeve intones, 'I want you to please welcome home ... Rush', and 'Bastille Day' just *explodes* through the speakers. More muscular, quicker, and pulsing with power, this is such a better version than the original that it becomes the definitive rendition. Lifeson's guitar sounds on fire, Lee and Peart attack their instruments with vigour, and the mix is excellent, capturing the raw spontaneity of the live performance with technical control. Lifeson's solo tone is exceptional, full-bodied and aggressive, and while the layering of instruments on the original is obviously absent, this stripped-down version is sleek and a brilliant opener to the album. The crowd's approval is well justified.

'Anthem' (4.56)

This, too, gets the no-holds-barred live approach, brimming with energy and confidence, and is again taken at a brisker pace than its studio counterpart. Lee is holding nothing back in the vocal department, his voice seemingly without an upper limit. Lifeson is not going to be upstaged by his friend, and his wah-wah-enhanced solo delivers the necessary goods in spectacular style, while Peart seems to be on a mission to destroy his drum kit.

'Fly By Night'/'In The Mood' (5.04)

'Fly By Night' is a far better song than 'In The Mood', and putting the two together as a mini medley is clunky. The inclusion of the latter merely emphasises the relative weakness of the debut album's material when put up against the melodic and lyrical power of the subsequent three albums. Why doesn't 'Between, Beneath, And Behind' appear as an alternative? Surely, 'Bacchus Plateau' deserves a viewing. Or why don't we take 'A Passage To Bangkok'? Three excellent shorter songs from the trio of Peart period albums. It's reasonable to assume that the majority of the fans preferred Rush 2.0 over the first incarnation, so why look so far back?

Notwithstanding this gripe, 'Fly By Night' again benefits from the heaviness of the live situation. Lifeson's high-energy solo is an instant highlight, with Lee simultaneously hammering his bass into submission. After the subsequent chorus, the song segues into 'In The Mood' at 2.08, and the dip in lyrical content immediately shows itself, even with Lifeson singing along for the chorus. Peart is constrained by the four-square boundaries of this very ordinary rocker, although he does his best with the occasional highly impressive roll or fill.

'Something For Nothing' (4.03)

The live setting enhances still further one of the heavier tracks from *2112*. Lee really goes for it with the vocals, but that is not to criticise Lifeson or Peart, who play as though their lives depended on it. Of course, the studio fade-out has to be re-engineered for an audience, and the song (and the first side of the double vinyl album) comes to a powerfully punchy close with some tight power-chord, bass and drum synchronisation after the final chorus.

'Lakeside Park' (5.04)

Geddy introduces this song with: 'We'd like to do something for you that's on *Caress Of Steel*. This is a song that Neil wrote the lyrics for, about a place not too far from where he was born, not too far from here as a matter of fact, it's called 'Lakeside Park'.

Lifeson's guitar copes well with the different moods of this gem of a song, switching with ease between the quieter, pretty sections and the harder-edged chord and solo passages. At the very close of the track, he makes a neat adjustment to his delay pedal setting to create a constantly repeating note, which then rises and then falls in pitch while in the background, the familiar synthesizer swirls of the introduction to 'Overture' are heard ...

'2112' (15.50)

'We'd like to do for you side one from our latest album, this is called '2112'.

Except, of course, we don't get the complete suite of songs; 'Discovery' and 'Oracle – The Dream' are absent. For the first-time listener to the tale, this disrupts the narrative. That aside, 'Overture' and 'The Temples Of Syrinx' are even more brutal and committed than their studio counterparts. 'Presentation's contrasts are suitably seismic with an explosive instrumental section, and 'Soliloquy' maintains its moody atmosphere right up till Lifeson rips his solo from the stratosphere. The closing 'Grand Finale' is magnificently up-tempo and monumental in its execution.

'By-Tor And The Snow Dog' (11.58)
The energy levels here don't quite match the audience-enhanced performances of the previous tracks. The long instrumental section does, however, really allow the trio to stretch out and create intriguing sound worlds, especially in the highly atmospheric 'Aftermath' section. Peart's drumming is, almost inevitably, exceptional throughout this live version, which is over two minutes longer than the original.

'In The End' (7.13)
Although at this stage in the band's career, Lifeson didn't deploy an acoustic guitar live, the absence of the pretty 12-string from the opening section of the song is not to its detriment. He uses a pleasing combination of a clean tone, a chorus pedal and reverberation to create a suitable contrast before his overdriven rock chords enter proceedings with a vengeance.

The overlaid funky-sounding second guitar part on the studio version (1.55 – 2.07) is here played by Lee in the upper reaches of the bass fingerboard before descending down to give substantial weight to the rhythm section. The overall tempo of this version is slightly slower than the original.

'Working Man'/'Finding My Way' (14.56)
While 'Working Man' rightly has 'instant classic' status stamped right through it, the same cannot be said for either 'Finding My Way' or 'What You're Doing'. Perhaps it was felt that the inclusion of two epics was enough for one live album. Possibly, it was a case of not totally abandoning their debut just because they had progressed so far so quickly. Whatever the reason, all three tracks are enhanced by Peart's percussive inventiveness and technical skill. While 'Working Man' would rightly remain in the band's set list, the decision to let the lesser songs gracefully slip into obscurity was a wise one. By the time the band's next live album rolled around (1981's *Exit Stage Left*), not even 'Working Man' made the cut as Rush were riding the waves of an incredible cycle of creativity which had culminated with *Moving Pictures*.

'Working Man' segues into 'Finding My Way' at 4.04 to an appreciative roar from the crowd, which may well be a studio 'enhancement'. 'Working Man' returns, mid-instrumental, at the seven-minute mark and runs through the rest of its length to what seems like its extended, slower and extremely heavy conclusion. This is interrupted by Lee announcing, 'Ladies and gentlemen, the Professor on the drum kit', and we are treated to a display of just what Peart is capable of (9.17 – 12.55).

I'm no fan of the drum solo as a part of the live ritual, but what we have here is someone doing things to drums that no other player (to my limited knowledge) had ever done before. The clever use of percussion and dynamics, alongside the fury of his playing, is as impressive as it is inventive. The solo finishes with a neat quote from the Oriental melody of 'A Passage To Bangkok'.

'What You're Doing' (5.40)

After a lengthy period of applause at the end of the previous track, 'What You're Doing' is an unusual choice for an encore. Again, other, more recent, and, crucially, *better* songs are available. As it is, we are dragged back to Led Zeppelin territory with only Peart's contributions making this comparative dinosaur worth a re-listen.

Quoted in *Anthem – Rush In The '70s*, Geddy said:

> Probably the funniest thing to do with that album was the way we ended it. We had this long applause, and in the end, we faded into the sound of Alex, Neil and myself in the parking lot clapping our hands. You really have to let the applause run to the end of the groove to hear it … and then we say, 'Okay, see you later', and then we get into a car and you hear the door slam and then we drive away.

Five years later, Rush would view *All The World's A Stage* as too rough, too raw, too basic. And so with their next concert release, *Exit Stage Left*, they went the other way and produced what Geddy would later describe as 'a fairly sterile live record'. Despite the supremely high quality of the material performed (there's only space for two songs from the first four studio albums), it's still *All The World's A Stage* that sounds like a proper 'live' album. Motto for the day? Don't let perfect be the enemy of the good!

A Farewell To Kings

Personnel:
Alex Lifeson: 6- and 12-string electric guitars, 6- and 12-string acoustic guitars, classical guitar, bass pedal synthesizer.
Geddy Lee: bass guitar, 12-string guitar, Mini Moog, bass pedal synthesizer, vocals.
Neil Peart: drums, orchestra bells, tubular bells, temple blocks, cowbells, wind chimes, bell tree, triangle, vibra-slap.
Recorded at Rockfield Studios, Monmouth, South Wales
Produced by Rush and Terry Brown
Engineered by Pat Moran
Released: 1 September 1977 on Mercury Records
All music composed by Lee & Lifeson with lyrics by Peart, except 'Closer To The Heart' by Peart and Talbot and 'Cinderella Man', with lyrics by Lee.
Chart positions: Canada: 11, US: 33, UK: 22

Touring went into overdrive from September 1976 to May 1977, with an increase in venue size and a further tipping of the scales from opening act to headliners, the highlight being two sold-out nights at the 7000-capacity Maple Leaf Gardens, Toronto. Despite this and the ever-increasing word of mouth from fans, radio stations still remained unresponsive. Whether it was the unusual and decidedly non-commercial style of their songs, Lee's 'acquired taste' voice or the intellectual heft of the lyrics, the band faced an uphill struggle to achieve airplay. Fast forward four short years and all that changed with *Moving Pictures*.

Rush was, however, making waves across the pond with significant support from Geoff Barton of the UK weekly music newspaper *Sounds*. Similarly, booking agent Neil Warnock, who had a reputation for getting American acts to break into Britain, noticed the band. He set an itinerary for a European tour, contacted SRO, and put himself forward as the band's international agent. Subsequently, an eight-day tour of major UK cities in June 1977 was arranged, with a single European date in Stockholm. The reaction to the band was far bigger and better than they expected. A loyal fan base was growing.

This increase in popularity led to a renegotiation of the record deal with Mercury, and in May 1977, Anthem Records was created. This was a label that could act as an umbrella for all the artists signed to SRO. *2112* had shown the rock world that Rush were determined to make music on their terms and be successful at it. *All The World's A Stage* cemented their growing reputation, and the anticipation amongst the converted was, 'What will they do now?'

What indeed? The band felt that their sound needed to be bigger but resisted the idea of recruiting an extra musician. Eschewing the previous *modus operandi* of writing while on tour, they rented a farmhouse for a few weeks in southern Ontario. Lee and Lifeson worked on new music while Peart crafted his lyrics. The trio would meet up later to compare notes, develop the strands, and repeat the process the next day until the new material was ready.

Forsaking Toronto Sound, the band initially tried recording in Electric Lady Studios New York but didn't feel the mood was right for the new material. Instead, they found themselves drawn across the Atlantic. Intending to use AIR Studios in London but finding it unavailable, the band, at Terry Brown's suggestion, decamped to Rockfield Studios in July 1977. Rockfield was part recording studio, part residential complex, set deep in the Welsh countryside, a block of former stable buildings in a quadrangle formation around the courtyard. In an interview with *Prog* magazine, Geddy said:

> *All The World's A Stage* was definitely something we used to buy us more time. We were doing well in Canada and things were getting more hectic. Frankly, we wanted to go somewhere where there were less distractions. Rockfield was our first residential record, so Terry suggested: why don't we look for a place where we could stay and work? We were all up for the adventure.

In *Contents Under Pressure,* Alex said:

> It really wasn't until *Kings* that we went somewhere and had dedicated writing time. And the interesting thing is that we were writing on an acoustic guitar, Geddy and I. I think all the stuff is written on an acoustic guitar, although they were rock songs.

The serious work began, and the new equipment (double neck guitars, two sets of bass Taurus pedals, and a Minimoog synthesizer) meant that the next album was going to be different again. As far as Rush was concerned, nothing was off-limits; everything was to be tried, and if it worked, it was 'in'. Once the recording was finished (in just three weeks), a further fortnight was booked at Advison Studios in London to complete the album.

In *Rush – Beyond The Lighted Stage,* Geddy recalled:

> These were the 'salad days' because we were transitioning and we could feel it. The world was expanding for us. We were starting to record in England, starting to get success in England, and to go over there and actually have a song in the charts ('Closer To The Heart') and play the Hammersmith Odeon; it was really gratifying because all of our heroes were English rock musicians so that gave us a tremendous amount of confidence.

The cover, another classic by Syme, shows a puppet king (portrayed by Josh Onderisin from the Ian Thomas Band) with a rictus smile, sitting on a throne, his crown at his feet as he slumps on the chair's arm. He is a marionette slumped in the outside ruins of a badly damaged building, in reality, a recently bulldozed warehouse in Buffalo. In the distance, 'the future', represented by a smokestack, high-rise office buildings, and a tall communications mast, is visible against a cloudy blue sky. The band name and album title are in an appropriate medieval-style font, which gives further emphasis to the sense of time and place. The gatefold sleeve included the lyrics and a moody black-and-white photograph of the trio taken by photographer Roger Stowell at a manor house not far from Rockfield. The back cover, all black with red lettering, carried on the puppet theme with a pair of discarded handles and strings. In the *Prog* magazine interview, Geddy said:

> That worked for us because it's a subtle theme that goes through part of the album that's all about loss. We have this thing; where are the next people we want to look up to going to come from? This is not an uncommon theme in Rush music – it's something that comes and goes with us. It's like everybody needs people to look up to, everybody needs people to emulate or be inspired by, and they're hard to find.

'A Farewell To Kings' (5.53)

In the same interview, Alex said:

> It (the title track) was a complex song to write. In many ways, it's simple and direct, but we could never accept that, so dropping a note here or inserting a weird note there made things more interesting for us and the listener. Odd time signatures were a great way to keep the listeners scratching their heads and counting on all fingers. 'Farewell' was quite a different piece for us because of the way it was structured, and then it comes in with a bang and there's this weird time signature going on. It's a tough song to play.

The title is taken from Act 1, Scene 1 of Shakespeare's *King Lear:* 'Fare thee well King. Sith thus thou wilt appear, freedom lives hence and banishment is here'.

Chapter Two in the annals of Rush begins in a most unexpected way. Rather than a bombastic guitar riff, or the unsettling swoop of a sci-fi synthesizer, we have a short, very pretty, Baroque-style classical guitar introduction with an added melody played on the MiniMoog. This was recorded in the courtyard of Rockfield, giving a wonderfully natural quality to the sound. It's a wonderful combination; the blend of the old (music) and the new (technology) creates something original, natural and timeless.

The first section has an unusual time signature structure. A bar of 3/4 is followed by three bars of 4/4 time. This is repeated and then developed with a further single bar of 3/4 two bars of 4/4, a bar of 5/4 and concluding with another bar of 4/4. As the tempo (approximately 124 crotchet beats per minute) remains constant throughout, these time changes don't disturb this elegant tranquillity.

Twenty-eight seconds in, synth and various percussive instruments join in. The structure is eight bars of 4/4 time (where a new melody and chord sequence is introduced) before reverting to a reprise of the initial theme with a bar of 3/4, three bars of 4/4, a bar of 3/4, two bars of 4/4, three bars of 5/4, and a single held chord. And that's just the first minute and ten seconds of the song.

After a brief pause, overdriven guitars, bass and drums then sweep in to claim the sonic world, and the recorded sound is just magnificent. There's clarity and space around each instrument, the mix is open and warm, and the overall effect is of a processional entrance, medium of tempo and proud of stride. This being Rush, of course, even this section isn't straightforward; four bars of 4/4 time are followed by three bars of 7/4, finishing off with a further two bars in 4/4. At 1.36, a new, slightly faster, sinewy guitar riff takes over, which is quickly joined by bass and drums as the first verse is unleashed.

Peart's lyrics are centred on corruption, greed, selfishness, and materialism. He describes the slow disintegration of the moral and social fabric of a society. In this dystopian time, the many have taken the path of least resistance, and are unable to tell right from wrong. Wisdom is no longer heeded, and consequently, tyrants disguised as kings rule a civilisation riven with hatred and fear. The castles of olden times represent what has been lost. Lee's portrayal of these powerful words is blooded and emotive.

The pre-chorus builds into the melodic and powerful chorus: 'Cities full of hatred, fear and lies, withered hearts and cruel tormented eyes. Scheming demons dressed in kingly guise, beating down the multitude and scoffing at the wise.' Threaded through this, Lifeson's soaring, simple lead motifs add much to the atmosphere. A second verse and pre-bridge section (2.40 – 3.14) are followed by the most complex instrumental section the band had composed thus far.

Set in 11/8 time and commencing with a funky, syncopated bass riff against some busy but light-touch drumming, this is a tour-de-force for the trio's musicianship and ambition. The guitar swoops and sours with an anguished, attacking tone, rising in a furious flurry of notes to a forceful, repeated single power chord rhythm, finally giving way to a more relaxed 4/4 time section of extended chords and more highly emotive solo work.

At 4.33, Lee returns with a further chorus, which is then repeated with different lyrics: 'Can't we raise our eyes and make a start? Can't we find the minds to lead us closer to the heart?' 'Closer To The Heart' was the working title for the album as it was one of the first songs to be written. Here, the tempo slows and the opening section (1.11 onwards) is reprised, ending on a single sustained chord from which the classical guitar reappears with a brief coda phrase, the song finishing on a single chord, bass note, and cymbal wash.

'A Farewell To Kings' is a stunning introduction to the newly expanding world of Rush. It gets overlooked with live album representation; 'bigger' tracks like 'Xanadu' and 'Cygnus X-1' get greater exposure, which is a shame, as this song is a quintessential example of Rush at this stage of their career. Imaginative instrumentation, advanced arrangements, powerful performance and wonderful words all combine to make this the perfect introduction to potential fans.

'Xanadu' (11.12)

Perhaps the most remarkable thing about the album's best track, and firm fan favourite, is that it was recorded *in a single take.*

Peart's original inspiration was the 1941 film *Citizen Kane,* directed by Orson Welles, which includes a line from Samuel Taylor Coleridge's poem *Kubla Khan*. Peart researched the poem and became more interested in it than the film, which led to the final lyric: the narrator seeking immortality in Xanadu. In the *Classic Rock* interview, Geddy recalled:

> 'Xanadu' was the first song that we did for that album, and we recorded it in the courtyard of Rockfield to get the natural echo. I was playing bass and also synthesizer – plugged into the studio, no amplifier. So, in one sense, it was completely meaningless for me to be out there with Alex and Neil. But I was wearing headphones so I could hear what I was playing, and that way, we could play together, play the part live, see each other and be connected.

The song can be broken down into 11 separate sections:

1: A sustained, low E on the synthesizer is decorated with Welsh bird song, violined guitar notes with additional delay, occasional temple block and wind chime effects, which build into a repeated climbing ostinato with a developing melody. At 1.17, the synth note is restated with the guitar tone becoming more intense, culminating in another arpeggiated sequence, this time descending into the lower register. Tubular bells are added as the synth tone becomes stronger. There is a real sense of pressure building here

2: At 1.50, a new, rotating, quaver-based guitar ostinato based around an E major scale appears from deep within the wind noise and birds chirruping. This is played in 7/8 time, the volume growing until the music just *explodes* at 2.04 with heavy chords (E major, G major, D major, and A major); the sequence is repeated three times, with impressive drum fills. This is an excellent section, full of power, melody, and style.

3: A new joyous-sounding section begins at 2.53, built around repeated five-bar phrases in 4/4 time. We are back in power trio mode; the synthesizer has disappeared, as has the birdlife. Peart's drumming is a joy here as Lifeson and Lee are locked together in rocking magnificence. This sequence is played four times, with the final time benefiting from an extended descent down the fingerboards for a further three bars until a single bar of 3/4 signals ...

4: At 3.36, a faster section based around a descending major chord sequence (E major, D major, B major, A major, and G major) appears in 7/4 time with a short and sweet melody added on the synthesizer. This section is repeated four times, with the mood calming at the A major chord in the final play-through, the chords becoming descending arpeggios of A(add 9), G6, Fsharp7 (sus4), and E major. A lighter feel section is dominated by lush guitar tones using a 'G6, Fsharp7 (sus4), A(add9), E major, G6, Fsharp7 (sus4), B(sus4)' chord progression, with some pretty bass lines and gentle percussion.

5. At 4.39, the song 'proper' starts with the classic arpeggiated chord sequence (E major, Fsharp7sus4). At this point mention must be made of the superb guitar sound captured by Terry Brown. Again, this was recorded in the courtyard at Rockfield, taking advantage of its natural ambience. Tubular bells are heard as a swaying rhythm begins.

6. 45% of the way through the track, the vocals appear. Lee's voice is soft here, as befits the lyrics and the relaxed feel of the music: 'To seek the sacred river Alph, to walk the caves of ice, to break my fast on honey dew and drink the milk of paradise…'

7. 5.23, and the music moves up several notches; the energy levels increase, matching the power of the guitars, bass and drums. The vocals have a harder edge, the band sound on fire, and this brisk section concludes with a short but spectacular roll around the drums before moving into a new section where, at a concert, the entire crowd would join Lee in singing the song's title at maximum volume.

8. Next is a return to the gentle sounds of the introduction. The synth returns over Lifeson's beautiful arpeggiated sequence, with the rhythm section kicking in behind the increasingly anguished vocals, which build to an emotive climax. Three power chords and the band revisit the section, which began at 2.53.

9. The anticipation and hope expressed earlier have now been replaced by bitterness and disappointment: 'A thousand years have come and gone and time has passed me by, stars stopped in the sky, frozen in an everlasting view'. The lyrics are bisected by a guitar scream to which a delay has been added before the realisation continues: 'Waiting for the world to end, weary of the night, praying for the light, prison of the lost – Xanadu.'

10. The pastoral texture returns, but the lyrics betray the feelings of this 'mad immortal man'. Lee bows out with a pained 'of paradise' as the music grows heavier and the tale concludes.

11. At 9.13 the instrumental coda begins with the highlight being a screaming guitar solo. There's nothing showy here, just pure emotion expressed through six strings as the music briefly subsides and the 7/8 ostinato makes a reappearance. A short calming and slowing of the music with a military-style drum rhythm is followed by a final mighty blast of power chords, and it's all over.

672 seconds of brilliance. Rush would, of course, have many recording highs in their studio career, but for many fans, 'Xanadu' is still the peak of the band in their full-on, prog rock-heavy period. The song's ability to transport the listener into Peart's mind and experience such a range of emotions from both Lee's vocals and the depth and mastery of the instrumental arrangements is stunning.

'Closer To The Heart' (2.54)

This is a track that encapsulates the album's theme and puts it, initially, in the style of a folk-protest song and was also the first time that Peart had collaborated with an 'outside' writer, Peter Talbot.

After all that drama and complexity, the second half of the album initially presents a more lyrical, melodic side of the band. 'Closer To The Heart' was also a surprise hit single climbing to 36 in the UK charts. And, for a band which eschewed commerciality, it's easy to see why.

The chiming 12-string guitar introduction, the beautiful melody, and the catchy chorus all attract and keep the attention, and the opening section all bring to mind 'Give A Little Bit' by Supertramp, also released in 1977. There is a joyfulness to the music, allied to the intelligence of the lyrics: 'And the men who hold high places must be the ones to start to mould a new reality closer to the heart.'

The second verse and the rest of the song up the electric ante with a gorgeous, soaring solo from Lifeson, which leads into the exhilarating final verse: 'You can be the Captain and I will draw the chart. Sailing into destiny, closer to the heart'. The repeated title leads into a riotous fade with all three players playing their (for want of a better word) hearts out.

'Cinderella Man' (Lee) (4.22)

Lee's solo composition was inspired by the 1936 film *Mr Deeds Goes To Town* in which Gary Cooper played 'a modest man from Mandrake' Falls who is both a tuba player and a poet. Upon inheriting a fortune, he decides to give it to the poor of New York City. As a result, he is hounded, and a court is convened to declare him insane. In the *Prog* interview, Geddy recalled:

> That song is really just about that movie and the kind of themes that the movie resonated with. It was my thing that I brought in, and Neil helped me clean it up a bit. One thing in Rush is that we've always allowed ourselves to go where we want to go as individuals and see how it flies. We all have to be behind it to use it. But there were no real boundaries in our band.

'Cinderella Man', the name given to Deeds by the Big Apple press, is an oddity; a heavy introduction features changes in time signature from two bars of 3/4 into a steady 4/4 groove and some virtuosic playing. By the time the verse arrives, a spirited acoustic guitar underscores the lyrics, giving the music a folky feel. When the rhythm section rejoins the fray, the music takes on a funk-lite style before the laid-back, melodic, acoustic-based chorus.

The instrumental section (2.26 – 3.16) features a superb, twisting, distorted guitar solo, with plenty of wah-wah flying between the stereo channels over a properly funky backdrop, which is reprised for the coda after the final lyrics.

'Madrigal' (2.34)

Hundreds of years ago, a poem set to music was termed a madrigal. This is a gentle love lyric with the most straightforward structure and instrumentation of the album. In effect, it's the calm before the incoming storm of the closing track. 'Madrigal' has never been performed live, belonging to the small category of songs intended solely as studio productions.

A sweet synth melody, a gently strummed guitar, simple bass, and minimal percussion act as a backdrop to the vocals. The arrangement and texture are a long way away from 'Tears' (*2112*). 'Madrigal' is a relaxed paean to the families the band has left back in Canada. The energy level lifts slightly when the drums join the texture for the final, more hopeful stanza: 'In vain to search for honour and in vain to search for truth. But these things can still be given your love has shown me proof.' This peaceful island of a song then fades away into the distance.

'Cygnus X-1: Book One: The Voyage' (10.28)

In the *'Classic Rock'* interview, Geddy thought:

> There was also a kind of continuation of '2112' in 'Cygnus X-1'. The one extends to the other. A lot of the musical themes in 'Cygnus X-1', like that whole spacey intro, are definitely connected back to '2112', although 'Cygnus X-1' is a bit more foreboding, I guess. But for sure, there would be no 'Cygnus X-1' without '2112'.

And after three concise, varied numbers the band return to the complex epic form to round off the album. Science fiction once again meets progressive hard rock in this tale of an astronaut who steers his spaceship on a voyage of discovery towards a black hole. The journey results in the ship's destruction and the astronaut's apparent demise, although the album sleeve intriguingly notes that this story is 'to be continued...' The track is a multi-faceted work, a stitching together of separate ideas and segments to form a whole which, while lacking the cohesion of 'Xanadu', still stands on its own as a complex, involving piece of music.

The opening section, 'Prologue', is initially pure atmosphere with a synthesizer, echoing tubular bells, and Terry Brown's studio-treated monologue setting the scene:

Left: The hair, the flares, the platform boots! This is Rush 1.0 featuring John Rutsey in a tasteful pink suit.

Below: Rush 2.0 – the 'new boy' is showcased in between the 'old guard'. (*Fin Costello/Redferns*)

Left: As debut singles go, 'Fade Away' rightly ... faded away. (*Moon Records*)

Right: As debut albums go, this self-titled one explodes with 'Working Man'. (*Moon Records*)

Right: Peart injects his flair into the Rush sound on *Fly By Night*. (*Mercury Records*)

Left: *Caress Of Steel* is the 'difficult (at times)' third album. (*Mercury Records*)

Above: Lee and Lifeson performing in November 1978, apparently playing in their sleep. Note the 'synth guitar'. (*Alamy*)

Left: The professor, 'professing'. (*Fin Costello/Redferns*)

Above: Rush saying *A Farewell To Kings*. Note the Fender Stratocaster rather than Lifeson's usual choice of a Gibson. (*Alamy*)

Below: Peart sans moustache, a permed Lifeson and Lee performing at the Seattle Center Coliseum in the late 1970s – the 1980s loomed... (*Alamy*)

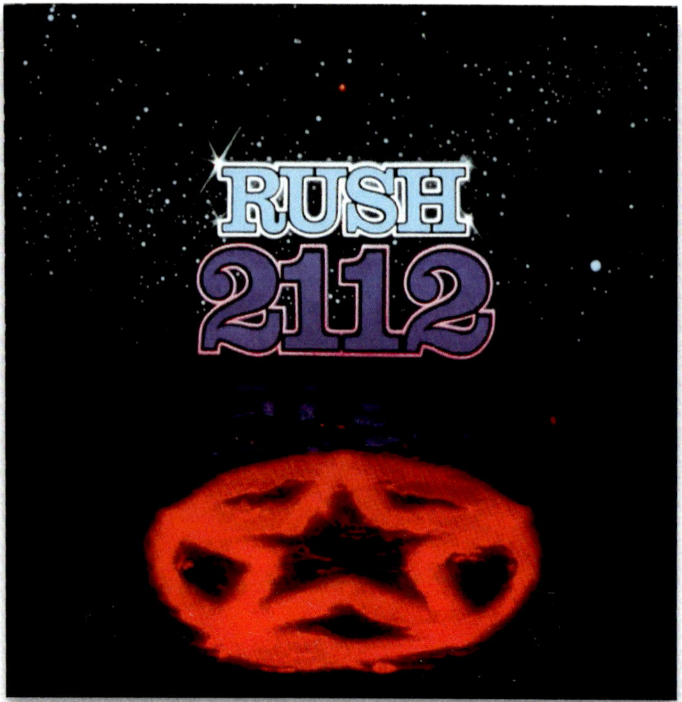

Left: *2112* can be considered the first masterpiece; it both saved and established the band as a force to be reckoned with. (*Mercury Records*)

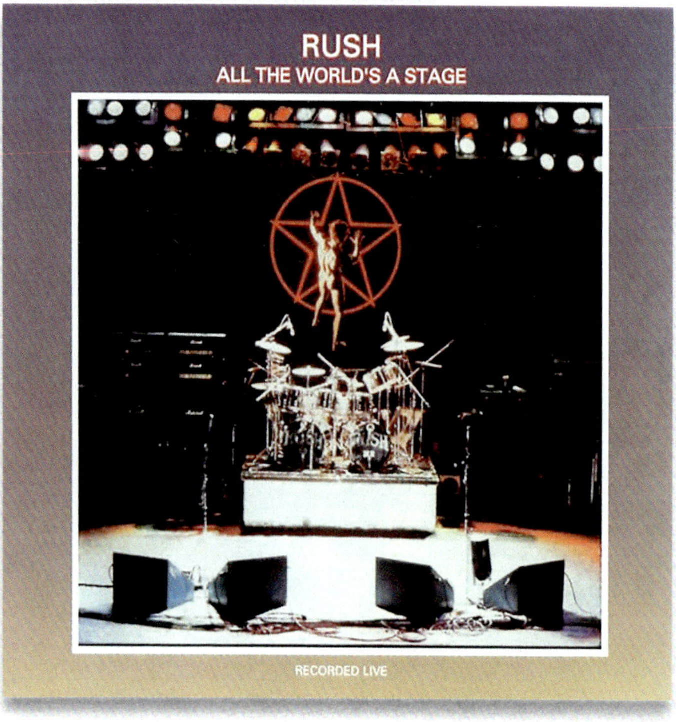

Right: The band's first raw and rocking live album, *All The World's A Stage* saw the end of Rush's first era. (*Mercury Records*)

Right: Keyboards enter the fray on *A Farewell To Kings* with magnificent, timeless results. (*Mercury Records*)

Left: The opening track on *Hemispheres* boasts the Alex Lifeson chord: 'Excuse me, sir. Have you seen my clothes?' (*Mercury Records*)

Left: *Permanent Waves* – a new decade, a new look and another fantastic collection of classic songs. (*Mercury Records*)

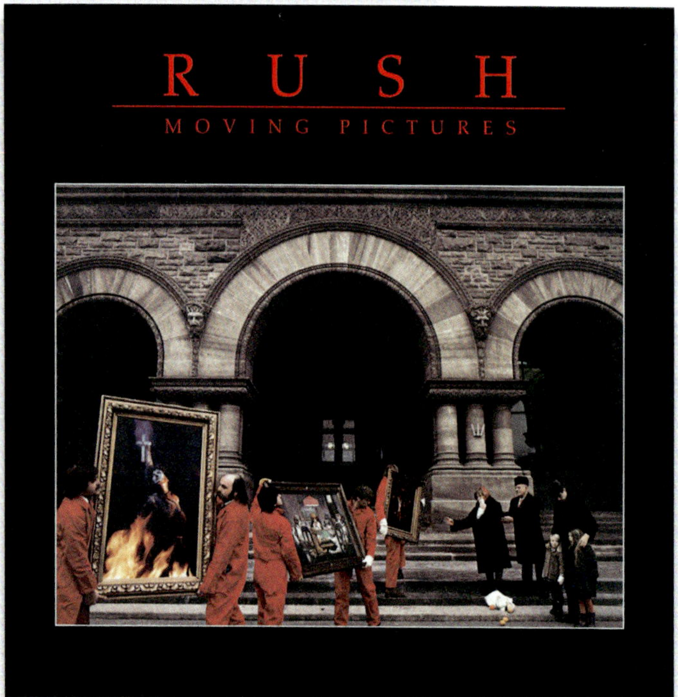

Right: *Moving Pictures* is the band's second masterpiece. If you only buy one Rush album… (*Mercury Records*)

Right: The wondrous songs on *Exit Stage Left* sound too polished to be genuinely live. (*Mercury Records*)

Left: *Signals* was the last album to feature Terry Brown as producer and heralded the beginning of another new style. (*Mercury Records*)

Left: Lee – apparently always the last in line when the band visit the hairdressers. (*Fin Costello/Redferns*)

Right: 'Hope you like our new direction' – the 1980s brought in a new contemporary look, sound and style, as seen here on the 'Subdivisions' music video.

Left: Neil Peart – universally recognised as being very, very good at hitting things with sticks.

Above: Lee and 'the keys'.

Left: The band's rebuke of *Sounds* magazine's review of their 1982 opus.

Above: Lifeson in full-on 'rock god' mode. (*Alamy*)

Above: Lee performing with Rush at the Forum on 15 June 1984. (*Alamy*)

Left: Peart looking ready to launch another attack on a completely innocent drum kit. (*Fin Costello/Redferns*)

Right: Terry Brown – the essential fourth member of the trio from 1974 to 1982.

Left: Hugh Syme – since *Caress Of Steel*, his artwork has defined Rush album covers.

Right: *Archives* – the first three albums repackaged in the wake of the success of *2112*. (*Anthem*)

Left: *Different Stages Live* is an absolute gem of a live performance. (*Anthem*)

> In the constellation of Cygnus, there lurks a mysterious, invisible force. The black hole of Cygnus X-1. Six stars of the Northern Cross, in mourning for their sister's loss, in a final flash of glory, nevermore to grace the night.

Into this spacey introduction emerges a classic bass riff, which grows closer and closer in the soundscape as the synthesizers and percussion gradually recede.

At 2.14, the drums join in, and at 2.26, an overdriven guitar adds further weight. The time signatures move between 6/8, 7/8, 6/8 and 4/4 in a repeating pattern until, at 2.58, a new theme is introduced. This incorporates power chords and octave tonics in 4/4 time before the music becomes more complex with a descending chordal passage interspersed with spectacular drum fills. This then breaks into a furious, short section in 12/8 before a rising chromatic-based scale drops into a lengthy rhythmic section which mixes two bars of 11/8 with a single bar of 12/8 time, over which a simple synth melody is introduced halfway through the nine repeats. The section closes on repeated Fsharp5 chords, and Lee's effects-laden voice begins the story.

Initially softly sung, voice and instruments *explode* with the next lyric: 'All who dare to cross her course are swallowed by a fearsome force.' The chord sequence from 2.58 is reintroduced as the astronaut's desire for exploration is described: 'Through the void to be destroyed, or is there something more? Atomised at the core, or through the Astral Door, to soar ...' At this point, the vocals are echoed and manipulated upwards in pitch as the next section begins.

The music here is new, not developing any of the ideas explored previously. Lifeson's guitar takes on a bright, power-pop feel, and his simple melody adds to the feeling of exuberance. The mood and tempo are upbeat, with the vocals capturing the anticipation of the voyage. The pace slows and the music becomes foreboding as the key changes from C major to C minor at 6.30 as the prospect of the journey resulting in tragedy is revealed: 'X-Ray is her siren song, my ship cannot resist her long, nearer to my deadly goal until the black hole gains control ...' with the rising chromatic-based scale from the 'Prologue' reappearing and an anguished, wah-wah based guitar solo.

Next is an instrumental depiction of the ship, the Rocinante, being devoured by the black hole. Repeated octaves, distant bells, and more spacey synth dominates with sudden brutal interjections from the bass and drums of the first riff from 'Prologue' until a sudden descent into an aggressive section in 11/8 before the full fury is unleashed, with Lee giving it his all over a restatement of the same music we heard in the latter part of the Prologue: 'Spinning, whirling, like a spiral sea unending, sound and fury drowns my heart, every nerve is torn apart ...'

This is where the track enters its transition phase between this album and the next. The gently strummed chords of C minor, D sharp minor and E minor are repeated to a fade. Behind this, the pulse of an irregular heartbeat is heard ...

'Cygnus X-1: Book One: The Voyage' is the most challenging track on 'A Farewell To Kings' both for the musicians and the listener. Whereas *2112* used an entire side of vinyl to develop its ideas, here, the band compress an awful lot into ten and a half minutes and set up the idea of an intriguing sequel.

In the *Prog* interview, Geddy mused on the significant use of synthesizers on the record:

> That's partly why I think *Farewell* was an important album for us. We did go into new territory with that record and it was a big step down a road, sonically, that we didn't really ever let go of. Two albums later, we'd make *Permanent Waves*. When you open that door of the synthesizer and the keyboard world, that was a Pandora's box for us, and after we'd opened it, all kinds of stuff came out over the next few years, but that's what made it glorious as a guy who was in the middle of it all. I was learning a lot. I was always challenged and I was very stimulated and the end result was 'A Farewell To Kings', so I guess it was a pivotal record in that regard.

Different Stages – Disc 3 – 20 February 1978

Fast forward two decades and Rush release a triple live CD, *Different Stages – Live,* on 10 November 1998, featuring two discs of recordings from their most recent tours for the *Counterparts* and *Test For Echo* albums. The third CD of the package was a concert at the Hammersmith Odeon, London, on 20 February 1978. Intended for a radio broadcast which never transpired, it's an audio snapshot of the band on their *Kings* tour, and is a fascinating listen.

The sleeve for the disc features a black and white photograph of the legendary venue proclaims 'Rush – plus Support', which would have been fellow Canadian prog rock group Max Webster. Groups of fans are seen hanging around outside the venue in the early evening. Hugh Syme clearly had a lot of fun compositing images of Lee (selling scalped tickets), Lifeson (being hauled away by two burly men dressed in white) and Peart (staring out of an upstairs window as if in jail) into the scene.

The recording was engineered by Terry Brown and, given the length of time the tapes had remained unattended, the sound is remarkably good. It is a warts-and-all experience and is all the better for it. This is the *genuine* live experience; no re-touching, no editing and no 'drop-ins'. This is a historical document of just how good Rush were at transporting their carefully crafted rock music onto the stage with electrifying results.

'Bastille Day' (5.08)
A fade-in of some orchestral music and an ecstatic crowd response give way to a full-bore power trio attack of one of their outstanding songs. The overall sound is a *little* on the ragged side, but this is easily overwhelmed by the pace, passion, and precision of the performance.

'By-Tor & The Snow Dog' (4.59)
The energy is maintained with this brisk rendition of the band's first multi-part song. The track segues at the end of the 'Of The Battle' subsection '7/4 War Furore' into the opening synthesizer note of…

'Xanadu' (12.32)
… a huge cheer greets Lee's announcement: 'We'd like to do something for you from our *Kings* album, this is called 'Xanadu', and the atmospheric introduction to, arguably, the band's best composition of the 1970s begins. And, given that this is an untouched-up version, the skills of all three musicians in creating such evocative moods live is highly impressive. Another loud cheer is heard as Lifeson's iconic, circling ostinato begins

'A Farewell To Kings' (5.53)
This is a rare but very welcome outing for this killer title track. The classical guitar introduction has Lee embellishing his pretty keyboards with various musical ornaments before the full might of the heavy rock returns with power

and purpose. The complex instrumental section is particularly breathtaking in a live setting, while the classical guitar coda is played on the electric; there's no time for a switch between instruments.

'Something For Nothing' (4.01)
The anthemic album closer from '2112' gets another full-blooded live rendition, with Lee pushing his voice to the absolute limits of its range.

'Cygnus X-1' (10.23)
The ghostly introduction is lifted from the album recording, the trio no doubt taking a short, well-deserved rest before tackling the complexities of the final track of *Kings*. The crowd get thoroughly into the syncopated bass riff and drum introduction, and when Lifeson joins in at 2.17, the sound is absolutely mighty.

Lee inserts pauses in his first, quiet vocals ('Invisible to tele ... scopic eye, In ... finity, the star that ... would not die'). The subsequent section is incredibly heavy, an example of just how the use of dynamics is so important in conveying music effectively.

'Anthem' (4.47)
After the evocative, self-faded ending of the chord sequence of 'Cygnus X-1', the band blast back in with this highlight of their very early years. Taken at a quicker tempo than the studio version, Lifeson's wah-wah enhanced mid-song solo is another plus point of the performance.

'Working Man' (4.00)
The career-launching classic gets another pounding and, given the location, Lee amusingly changes the lyrics of the second verse from 'ice-cold beer' to 'Watney's Red Barrel'.

For those unfamiliar with the taste of this now happily defunct English beer, the recipe can be replicated by taking a handful of mud, throwing it in a pint of rainwater, adding some salt, stirring vigorously and leaving to stand outside for at least two winters. You can thank me if you recover.

The instrumental is cut short at the end of the simultaneous 'octave riff' section, segueing straight into ...

'Fly By Night' (2.04)
... another 'faster than the studio' performance that has Lee syncopating his familiar vocal lines, the song following the *All The World's A Stage* template by moving straight into ...

'In The Mood' (3.34)
... and, at this stage in the band's astonishing creative ascendancy, it's strange that this basic, bar-room rocker still warrants a place in their live set. What

about some 'Changes'? 'Best I Can', whilst still being a second-division level song, could have received a live airing. Perhaps Rush felt they still needed to pay their respects to the debut, even though the majority of that album is so out of style with the direction in which they were heading.

There's an impressive 'big-rock' ending with Peart every drum and cymbal in front of him very hard indeed, a sustained chord, and a busy Lifeson manic solo before the track comes to a tight end.

'Cinderella Man' (5.09)
Another welcome inclusion, 'Cinderella Man' was the encore number for the tour. Here, the rhythmic acoustic guitar of the verses is replaced by some overdriven, funked-up electric strumming. The live setting robs the song of some of its dynamic light and shade, but this remains another fiery performance, the band on their way through the roof.

This 'bonus' disc is, of course, aural catnip for fans who first discovered the band in the 1970s. Furthermore, like *All The World's A Stage* before it, it *sounds* live because this recording is very much the 'real deal'. It's great to hear a single performance, minor glitches and all, as it happened.

Hemispheres

Personnel:
Alex Lifeson: 6- and 12-string electric and acoustic guitars, classical guitar, Roland guitar synthesizer, Taurus pedals
Geddy Lee: bass guitar, Mini Moog, Oberheim synthesizer, Taurus pedals, vocals
Neil Peart: drums, orchestra bells, bell tree, timpani, gong, cowbells, temple blocks, wind chimes, crotales
Recorded at Rockfield Studios, Monmouth, South Wales
Produced by Rush and Terry Brown
Released: 29 October 1978 on Mercury Records
All music composed by Lee & Lifeson, with lyrics by Peart
Chart positions: Canada: 14, US: 47, UK: 14

> It could be a meisterwerk (but it's more like a terrible mistake).

Thus typed Geoff Barton in his review of *Hemispheres* in *Sounds*. In its conclusion, he believed that Rush had 'become too ambitious for their own good'.

In Europe, the albums prior to *Kings* had only been available on import; *Kings* was the first to be selected by Mercury's parent company, Phonogram, as a bona-fide European release, doing extremely well. A subsequent British tour in the spring of 1978 quickly sold out, and the pressure was on the trio to produce the goods again to capitalise on this breakthrough. As a 'stop-gap' cash-in, Mercury re-released the band's first three albums as a triple set entitled *Archives* in April 1978.

The band returned to Rockfield. Unusually, they did not have enough material, and so an old Mill House, near to the studio was rented for three weeks to complete the compositions before going into the studio.

The musical elephant in the room was, of course, the continuation of the story set in motion with 'Cygnus X-1'. Rush had made a rod for their own back, inserting 'To be continued…' on the inner sleeve of *Kings*. They didn't *have* to conclude the saga with the *next* album. Peart, however, *was* committed to finishing the saga. For fans eagerly awaiting the band's next album, it would have been strange if the tale had not been continued. 'Don't worry, everyone, we'll get back to it later!' In *Contents Under Pressure,* Geddy recalled:

> It was such an exceedingly difficult album to record – because we spent weeks writing, and we were experimenting with new keyboards, and it was an ambitious record rhythmically with odd time changes and stuff like that. It's probably the most complex record we've ever made. When we got to Rockfield, finally, after writing this stuff, we wanted to record as much live off the floor as we could, as much in one piece as we could.
>
> When we finally got all the vocals down and then started mixing it at

> Advison, we couldn't get the mix; everything sounded wrong. And that's when we moved studios again and moved to Trident Studios, where it all came together; it was just the right room for it. But at every stage of that record, there were unseen problems, also worsened by the fact that we were months away from home in England. Our families were becoming just, you know – a rumour.

It is the inevitable continuation of 'Cygnus X-1', which, obliquely, informs the album cover. A naked man (the symbol of *2112* made flesh was actually a Toronto-based ballet dancer). Facing away from us, he points at a bowler hat-wearing businessman across the surface of a floating brain. In a neat symmetry, the smartly dressed model is Bob King, who posed as the 'Star Man' for the *2112* cover. Two other brains are nearby, all suspended over a desert against a cloudless blue sky. This was the first time that Lee, Lifeson and Peart would be referenced through a trio of items in the artwork by Syme. Future examples would include the red balls of *Hold Your Fire* (1987) and the floating femurs and walking wishbones of *Roll The Bones* (1991).

The cover comes across as a mixture of Salvador Dali, Magritte, and Hypgnosis, and neither the band nor the artist were particularly enamoured with the end result. With Rush in Wales and Syme in Canada, communications were haphazard, and wires got crossed. In effect, the whole project was a bit of a 'rush' job. The inner gatefold presented the lyrics, and once again, fans were thrown a curve ball. The final track was a nine-and-a-half-minute instrumental. In between these two substantial pieces were two shorter numbers.

Peart found inspiration in the book *Powers Of Mind* written by George Goodman (1930 – 2014) in 1975, under the pseudonym of Adam Smith, which compared psychology to religion. Peart decided upon a mythical dispute between the gods Apollo (representing reason, the businessman) and Dionysus (depicting love and, apparently, nudity) to rule the 'fate of man'. This was presented as an allegory for the battle between the head (or, more accurately, the left brain as the centre of reason and objectivity) and the heart (represented by the right hemisphere, the home of intuition and subjectivity). Into this fight would appear the remains of the astronaut from 'Cygnus X-1' to provide a balance between the warring factions.

Hemispheres is Rush at peak-prog. From the six-section song suite occupying the entire first side of the original vinyl to the ridiculously impressive (or, for the critics, just ridiculous) lengthy instrumental which closes the record, the band's talents are on full display. While the album lacks a track matching 'Xanadu's epic stature, the ideas are compelling and the musicianship and scope of the band's ambition and self-confidence in their approach are similarly impressive.

However, *Hemispheres* was the last time the band would write side-long epics. They feared becoming formulaic. The 'Rush brand' of progressive rock would progress into something more concise, focused and future-facing. As a last hurrah, then, is 'Hemispheres' indeed a 'meisterwerk or a mistake?' Let's find out…

'Cygnus X-1 Book II – Hemispheres' (18.09)

'I: Prelude' (0.00 – 4.30)

In effect this is an overture featuring many of the musical themes which appear later in the suite. 'Prelude' opens with a whoosh of synthesizer and the first appearance of what would become known in rock guitar circles as the 'Lifeson chord', an F#7(sus4). This appears frequently throughout the track, the first minutes of which dispense with subtly and dynamics and hit the ears with a heavy rocking intensity. Time signature changes abound; 12/8, 9/8, 3/4, 7/8, and 4/4 all feature in various combinations until, two minutes in, the mood changes dramatically.

At 1.58, a pretty ostinato using open string 'natural' guitar harmonics is accompanied by a sustained synth note and busy, light percussion. (This is a technique Lifeson would further develop and deploy as part of the introduction to 'Red Barchetta' on *Moving Pictures*). Bass punches are soon joined by a driving drum rhythm with a single brief moment of delightful contrast; at 2.36, there is the isolated sound of a triangle being struck, which is possibly the only time the instrument has featured so prominently on a rock record. Then the full power trio sound returns.

To conclude the section Lee finally sets the scene of what is to come: 'When our weary world was young, the struggle of the Ancients first began. The Gods of Love and Reason sought alone to rule the fate of man. They battled through the ages, but still, neither force would yield. Their people were divided, every soul a battlefield …' Fans expecting a direct continuation of the story established with 'Cygnus X-1' were instantly wrong-footed. How was *this* linked to what had gone before? The following three songs did nothing to alter that perception.

'II: Apollo – Bringer Of Wisdom' (4.31 – 7.01)
'III: Dionysus – Bringer Of Love' (7.02 – 9.06)

These two songs are virtually identical musically but with differing lyrics, separated by one of the few actual guitar solos in the piece (6.26 – 6.54). Peart's idea of showing equally balanced yet competing forces comes unstuck here as the repetition of the musical themes becomes wearing.

Lyrically, it's a tale of two halves. On Apollo's recommendation, the people learn of 'truth and understanding, wit and wisdom fair'. Food, shelter and fire are provided and yet, despite living in cities in 'grace and comfort', the people become dissatisfied. Therefore, after a consultation with the wise men, they cross the Bridge of Death (not available on Google Maps) to seek an alternative lifestyle.

Dionysus is a very different kettle of philosophical fish. Love, feelings, laughter and music are all on offer, and as the 'chains of reason' are discarded, the people's 'prison disappears.' Suitably swayed, the cities are soon empty, and life transfers to the forests with food and wine 'aplenty'. The contented population become less impressed when winter comes, 'bringing wolves and cold starvation', and despair sets in. What to do? There's just no pleasing some civilisations. Picking narrative nits, the original Dionysus represented wine, not love; that was Venus's role. Or perhaps it was a very early form of job sharing.

Had Apollo's viewpoint been represented by a more regimented style of composition, with Dionysus' stance being given freer (maybe – dare I type it – jazzy?) musical rein, the differences between the two ideologies would have been much more effectively illustrated. No doubt the intention was, of course, to show the two contrasting philosophies fighting for dominance, with no apparent resolution possible. But the joint 'Apollo' and 'Dionysis' matching themes take up four and a half minutes of the 18-minute suite, and after a time, this repetition starts to feel laboured.

As 'La Villa Strangiato' shows, there was no shortage of creativity within the band, and such a 'musical personality' contrast would have maintained a freshness to the tale at this point. That said, this is still impressive music played with intensity and sung with passion, which segues effortlessly into the 12/8 and 9/8 groove of …

'IV: Armageddon – The Battle Of Heart And Mind' (9.07 – 12.12)

… over which Lifeson plays a series of flowing, heavily flanged, falling and rising melodic phrases flowing between the stereo channels. Lee's voice is right at the top of his range: 'The Universe divided as the heart and mind collided, with the people left unguided for so many troubled years. In a cloud of doubts and fears, their world was torn asunder into hollow hemispheres.'

In the midst of all this, the narrative switches abruptly to the perspective of the long-missing astronaut and his ship: 'My Rocinante sailed by night on her final flight. To the heart of Cygnus' fearsome force, we set our course, spiralled through that timeless space to this immortal place.'

So it's taken eleven minutes, but finally, a connection between Books I and II is established. A simple synth note with some fabulous power chords leads up to the link of the musical threads with the eight rising notes that accompanied the lyrics from 'Book 1' appearing ('Until the black hole – gains control') and being repeated. The song concludes with three sustained heavy power chords, the decaying sound of which blends into the haunting chord sequence that left us in suspense at the end of *Kings*.

'V: Cygnus – Bringer Of Balance' (12.13 – 17.03)

A sustained synthesizer chord takes over from the guitar, and two brief excerpts from 'Book I' are heard in the distance. Then the voice of the astronaut appears: 'I have memory and awareness, but I have no shape or form. As a disembodied spirit, I am dead and yet unborn. I have passed into Olympus as was told in tales of old, to the city of Immortals, marble white and purest gold.'

As well as this section being a welcome change of texture from the hard rocking complexity of the previous 12 minutes, this is also the first time we have heard Lee's 'soft' voice. He sounds far more comfortable singing at this pitch than elsewhere in the track. Witnessing the ongoing battle (explosion sound effects are heard in the background), the entity feels 'a silent scream begin inside', and the music suddenly explodes into a sequence reminiscent of the opening rock section of *A Farewell To Kings*: 'Then all at once the chaos ceased, a stillness fell, a sudden peace. The warriors felt my silent cry and stayed their struggle, mystified.'

Again, multiple time signature changes are unleashed; 4/4, 3/4, 2/4, and 7/8 all get a look-in. Witnessing the destruction their battle has wrought on the world below them, the Gods call a truce. 'They sat a while in silence, then they turned at last to me: 'We will call you Cygnus, the God of Balance you shall be".

At this point (15.52), the opening chords of the 'Prelude' are repeated. Then, the mood turns celebratory, with a major key chord sequence rocking out against a solid 12/8 rhythm, with Lee and Peart having the most fun against Lifeson's powerful accompaniment. The song comes to a huge ending after the briefest of pauses with a massive A major chord and a gong. As this fades away, another island of peace appears ...

'VI: The Sphere – A Kind Of Dream' (17.04 – 18.09)

This brief coda to 'Book II' features a gentle-voiced Lee, a 12-string guitar and a simple synthesizer. The lyrics emphasise the intent of the composition; a balance of heart and mind is essential, and this is neatly summed up in one of Peart's wordplay lines: 'Sensibility, armed with sense and liberty' is the way forward.

'The Sphere – A Kind of Dream' is a pretty, melodic piece and brings 'Hemispheres' to a positive conclusion. The last of the side-long epic tales doesn't *quite* have the impact of '2112', the melodic, cinematic magnificence of 'Xanadu', or the stark musical contrasts of 'Cygnus X-1'. However, 'Book II' stands up well in the Rush canon of work as an impressive feat, marrying the complexities of prog rock with the force of a power trio and lyrics which, if nothing else, give the listener pause for thought. In the *Classic Rock* interview, Geddy said:

> The title track was another side-long piece. It was, in a sense, a different version of '2112'. The notes were different, the story was different, but structurally we started feeling that we were repeating ourselves. So we thought, 'This isn't healthy for us. We've got to break out of that. We needed a new direction,' and we found it with *Permanent Waves*.

'Circumstances' (3.44)

As if to shake themselves free of the musical shackles in which they felt entangled, 'Circumstances' immediately states the case for the change that was coming. Short, precise, and punchy, 'Circumstances' is almost the complete antithesis to 'Hemispheres'.

The lyrics of the first verse allude to Peart's time in London, with the chorus broadening the narrative to conclude that no one is in complete control of their destiny and that circumstances, both past and present, offer and remove opportunities. The refrain 'Plus ca change, plus c'est la meme-chose' is immediately translated: 'The more that things change, the more they stay the same'.

Despite its brevity and relatively standard rock song formula (introduction, verse and chorus, a second verse and chorus, an instrumental followed by a third chorus). 'Circumstances' still moves through several time signatures and maintains the intensity of performance that characterised the title track. The instrumental section (2.11 – 3.12) is an impressive minute of melodic complexity, with an initial synthesizer-led melody being a throwback to the pastoral textures that characterised parts of 'A Farewell To Kings' and 'Xanadu'. Powerful guitar, bass, and drums crash in with a full-blooded heavy rock assault to bring the music back to the final chorus.

'Circumstances' is an overlooked gem and a compositional marker for the band's future, one which would be repeated with varying degrees of success for much of the rest of their career.

'The Trees' (4.44)

The second song written for the album, and a reminder that *Kings* and *Hemispheres* are really two halves of the same whole, the graceful classical guitar introduction was again recorded in the Rockfield courtyard. Lee provides fluid, flanged bass lines under his vocals while birds are heard in the background.

The lyrics are, however, not one of Peart's finest moments, the writer admitting that he took inspiration from a cartoon he saw where a group of trees took on human characteristics. The words can be interpreted as a representation of the civil rights movement, using the oppressed small Maples taking their campaign to the taller Oaks, who are blocking their sunlight. So far, so Sixth Form poetry competition. In the magazine *Modern Drummer Legends,* Peart admitted:

> Lyrically, it's a piece of doggerel. I certainly wouldn't be proud of the writing skill of that. What I would be proud of in that is taking a pure idea and creating an image for it. Although, on the skill side of it, it's 'zero'. I wrote 'Trees' in about five minutes. It's simple rhyming and phrasing, but it illustrates a point so clearly. I wish I could do that all the time.

The good news is that forty seconds in, the tranquil opening mood is shattered by the arrival of the trio in full heavy rock mode. Everything sounds fantastic here; Lee's vocals soar, Lifeson's guitar is full and scything, and Peart hits everything *hard*. As an illustration of dynamic and textural contrast, this is superb. The sound calms again at 1.47 for the instrumental section.

The opening part of this is highly evocative of the forest setting. Over a soothing electric guitar arpeggio sequence, Lee plays a dreamy-toned synth melody as Peart adds rapid temple block runs. The mood darkens at 2.17; the time signature slides from 4/4 into 5/4, with a lower-pitched synth tone accompanied by percussive stabs. These increase in intensity until a medium-tempo bass and drum rhythm (still in 5/4) is established. Initially, Lee is at the forefront of the mix with an effective prog funk riff; Lifeson soon dominates the section with a wide-ranging, note-wrenching solo from 3.10 onwards. This builds to a crescendo at 3.29, the time signature moves into 3/4 and syncopated heavy guitar chords lead to an amusing rising six-note scale, which Peart mimics with a descending pattern on cowbells. This trick occurs four times with subtle variations, followed by a twice repeated new riff over two bars of 4/4 and a bar of 2/4.

Lee then resumes the story as the maples form a union to demand 'equal rights'. To prevent Oak oppression a 'noble law' is passed and 'the trees are all kept equal, with hatchet, axe, and saw.' 'The Trees' became a fan favourite and was featured in the band's setlist for years to come.

'La Villa Strangiato' (9.37)

In *Contents Under Pressure*, Geddy recalled the pressures the band put themselves under to achieve the best results possible. With reference to their longest instrumental work, he said:

> Even 'La Villa Strangiato' we wanted to record as one ten-minute piece. But we were also becoming perfectionists at this point and just didn't like the long pieces we were doing. They started to lose energy, so we finally compromised, and I think we recorded that song in three pieces, and then we glued them together.

This, for me, is Rush at their proggiest; seven time signatures, three different keys, eighteen chords, and many, many notes all create a unique piece which underlines its sub-title, 'An Exercise In Self Indulgence'. 'La Villa Strangiato' is a fantastically creative and original instrumental, much of which was inspired by Lifeson's frequent and vivid dreams. It covers many moods and textures and contains some of the band's finest playing. With no vocal commitments, Lee throws himself into intricate bass lines and supporting keyboard duties with *elan*. For his part, Peart shows just how interesting and involving a drum kit can be in the right hands, and Lifeson plays one of the best, most evocative solos of his career.

'La Villa Strangiato' is all over the place – in a *very* good way. The band seem to have so many competing musical ideas that rather than try and distil some of them down into more songs, they just go with this: nearly ten minutes of the most astonishing creativity. From its Spanish guitar introduction through the melodic rocking into Lifeson's magical solo and the cornucopia of musical intensity that follows it, the listener is never sure where the band are going next. Whatever 'La Villa Strangiato' 'is', it's certainly never boring.

'I: Buenos Nochas, Mein Froinds' (0.00 – 0.27)
Based very loosely on the song 'Gute Nacht, Freunde' by the German composer Alfons Yondrascheck, this is an impressive piece of solo classical guitar playing which starts with great subtlety before a furious Spanish-sounding flurry of semiquavers, concluding on a strummed F major chord which blends into ...

'II: To Sleep, Perchance To Dream ...' (0.28 – 1.59)
... some delicate guitar arpeggios based around a C(add9) chord set up a hypnotic drone atmosphere. Joined by a pleasant synthesizer melody and gradually building percussion, there is a happy, upbeat feel which is maintained throughout the section's 59 bars. Gradually, the synthesizer disappears as guitar, bass and drums keep the momentum up as the volume crescendos into ...

'III: Strangiato Theme' (2.00 – 3.15)
... savage power chords and a drop down into A major with a syncopated chord pattern and rapid six-note semi-quaver descending melody, which is played four times before an anthemic 'chorus' (of sorts) at 2.13 – 2.25. The heroic mood continues with a new guitar-led melody with alternating C5 and Fsharp5 power chords. This entire section is repeated and the band just sound on *fire*, brimming with confidence, technical excellence, and a sense of fun; three highly talented musicians having the time of their lives in a sandpit of their own making.

'IV: A Lerxst In Wonderland' (3.16 – 5.49)
The mood changes abruptly here. 'Lerxst' is Lifeson's nickname (Lee is 'Dirk' and Peart is 'Pratt') and this is the guitarist's showcase as he gives us a tour of his 'Wonderland' in magnificent style.

The time signature moves from its solid 4/4 rock basis into a less comfortable 7/4 and sustained chords of F major and A major signal a new section. Dynamics reduce as bass and drums roll back the intensity, and Lifeson just begins to *fly*. In an interview with *Guitar World* magazine, he admitted that this section was an overdub, but despite this, the original recording is *just* discernable in the far background.

His solo (3.40 – 5.14) is a masterclass in phrasing, tone, and feel. Starting with some ghostly, violined notes, he gradually builds the intensity with elements of blues merging into more anguished hard rock tones. At 4.28, he really digs in and produces some of his best playing to date, the pace becoming more frenzied as the bass and drums crescendo with additional synth in the background.

A spectacular rapid run down the fretboard leads into a low-range ostinato, which grows in menacing volume, with exceptional drumming bringing even greater urgency to the section.

Suddenly, it's time for ...

'V: Monsters!' (5.50 – 6.09)

Here the music is angry, energetic and at double the speed of the previous section. The 'Monsters!' riff, lifted from Raymond Scott's 1937 jazz melody 'Powerhouse', is played four times in 7/8 time before crashing into 4/4 for a further four bars.

The melody is repeated a further four times, an octave higher on the guitar, matched by bass and spectacular drums.

'VI: The Ghost Of Aragon' (6.10 – 6.45)

Maintaining the furious energy level, Lee plays a brief semiquaver jazz-influenced bass solo over two bars before Lifeson powers in with a series of syncopated, chromatically descending power chords covering the octave down from A5. The jazz feel continues with Peart's interjections and a shortened repeat of the power chord descent. At 6.30, a rising crotchet scale over two bars has echoes of the 'until the black hole takes control' excerpt from 'Cygnus X-1'. A brief flurry of drums leads us into ...

'VII: Danforth And Pape' (6.46 – 7.26)

Named after the intersection of two streets not far from where Lifeson and Lee lived, 'Danforth and Pape' is a relentless pattern of two bars of C major and two bars of F sharp major. Lifeson effortlessly throws in another spectacular solo, culminating in a repeated rising melody.

'VIII: The Waltz Of The Shreves' (7.27 – 7.53)

This short section begins with single crotchet notes played in 9/8 time. Effective delayed notes appear in the quaver rests for three bars before moving into a rolling arpeggio pattern. The music lands on a straightforward shuffle rhythm, which, given all the complexity and musical dexterity which has gone before, is surprising.

'IX: Never Turn Your Back On A Monster' (7.54 – 8.03)

It is over this relatively simplistic rhythm that the 'Monsters!' theme returns in 12/8 time. Moody and menacing, it morphs quickly into ...

'X: Monsters! (Reprise)' (8.04 – 8.16)
Moving back into a fast four, Lifeson reprises the theme, firstly at the same pitch and then an octave higher over this eight-bar section. Acknowledging the ownership of the 'Monsters!' melody, Rush made a one-off 'penance payment' for the rights to use Scott's music.

'XI: Strangiato Theme (Reprise)' (8.17 – 9.21)
The tempo increases from 132 to 154 beats per minute for this reprise section, which is marginally faster than when it first appeared.

'XII: A Farewell To Things' (9.22 – 9.37)
The title of this final section is, in retrospect, a nod towards the musical future the band were preparing for, one of streamlining and a drive towards realism aided by ever-developing technology.

Consisting of the four repeats of the 'Monsters!' riff, the chromatic power-chord descent from 'The Ghost Of Aragon', another two bar jazzy bass flurry, a sudden finish on C major up-ends the listener's expectations, if they were anticipating some kind of 'big-rock' ending. Unconventional, spectacular and surprising, 'La Villa Strangiato' is all this and more.

Oh, and by the way, Geoff? This track and the entire album? Masterful work…

In *Contents Under Pressure,* Neil provided an analysis of the band's two most recent albums:

> *A Farewell To Kings* and *Hemispheres* are very much of a period. And, in fact, they represent a period to themselves. It was with *A Farewell To Kings* that we started with a lot of the textural experimentation. And we took it to its apogee absolutely with *Hemispheres*, then decided that we wouldn't do that anymore. *Hemispheres* was the end … we didn't want to do side-long pieces, the overblown arranging, anymore. We agreed at the time even then that we were done with that, and we, of course, moved on with *Permanent Waves* – more in an evolutionary way, but yet it was more than that.

Rush's desire for constant exploration, experimentation and 'progress' in its broadest musical sense meant that treading musical water was never going to be an option. The first step in this new, compact direction was to be as bold as it was successful.

Permanent Waves

Personnel:
Alex Lifeson: electric and acoustic guitars, Taurus pedals
Geddy Lee: bass guitar, Oberheim synthesizers, Taurus pedals, vocals
Neil Peart: drums, timpani, timbales, orchestra bells, tubular bells, wind chimes, bell tree, triangle, crotales
Erwig Chuapchuaduah: steel drums ('The Spirit Of Radio')
Hugh Syme: piano ('Different Strings')
Recorded at Le Studio, Morin Heights, Quebec, Canada
Produced by Rush and Terry Brown
Released: 14 January 1980 on Mercury Records
All music composed by Lee & Lifeson with lyrics by Peart, except 'Different Strings' by Lee
Chart positions: Canada: 3, US: 4, UK: 3

The *Hemispheres* tour had been the first one to turn a profit. This was a problem of the band's making; Rush always wanted their fans to see and hear the best show possible, and as the size of venues and crowds grew, so did staging and presentation costs. In June 1978, the tour concluded, and after six weeks rest the trio reconvened at Lakewoods Farm, north of Toronto, to work on new material. Always open to fresh ideas and influences, Rush's eighth release would be less about breaking with their past as much as catching up with the then present.

In *Chemistry,* Peart said:

> When more thoughtful bands like Talking Heads came out and later the New Romantics I embraced it totally. It was an irresistible force at that point; it was just rock music that could call itself new wave. We started to feel more assured as both musicians and songwriters. We were able to look at a song as just a song and no longer felt compelled to overdress the music in order to hide inadequacies. We are a sponge and we don't try to hide that. We're perfectly open to new influences all the time and love them, and love being inspired by them.

A new decade, a cleaner look, and a more concise approach to songwriting signalled a band moving with the times. For the first time, Rush showed signs of approaching the rock mainstream, albeit on their own terms. *Permanent Waves*, while retaining many of the elements of the prog rock genre, has a more focused, forward-looking approach. No side-long epics, no fantasy lyrics; this was the sound of the band re-inventing themselves for the decade ahead. In keeping with the ethos of being a *progressive* rock band, Rush composed songs that were more aligned with the new musical and realistic physical world around them. In an interview with *Sounds* magazine in December 1982, Neal said:

> ...(it) had more to do with writing about people and less about ideas. *Permanent Waves* was probably our first album that was in touch with reality – it was all about people dealing with technology instead of people dealing with some futuristic fantasy world or using symbols for people. Now, I'm trying to make those symbols into real people and real conflicts in real people's lives. I still want to write about ideals; I'm not interested in writing about the sewer of life.

The band moved into Le Studio to begin recording, with the entire experience being more relaxed than the *Hemispheres* sessions. Once completed, well on schedule, the album was finalised a week later back at Trident Studios in London. In the *Classic Rock* interview, Geddy remembered the experience of recording back in Canada:

> It was the first time we recorded at Le Studio in Morin Heights, Quebec – this beautiful mountain retreat. We recorded in this room that had giant picture windows. After recording all those years in bunkers, it was such a refreshing change. And I think that contributed to the 'up' vibe of that whole record. That album came together really quickly, and to this day, it's one of the most pleasurable recording sessions we've ever had. We knocked it off in five or six weeks, and that was it. Done.

In *Limelight – Rush In The '80s* by Martin Popoff, Geddy considered the definition of what a progressive rock band should be:

> It's much more interesting to try to take that idea of being progressive and not do it in a way that people expect you to be progressive. What is a progressive band? Oh, you do a concept album that has space involved, and here's a long instrumental portion; here's an overture. That, to me, seemed less interesting than saying, okay, let's do ten individual songs and each of them can be a mini concept unto itself. And it's okay that there's a thread that connects all these concepts, and the thread is the concept, right? It's not the repeating melody lines or the repeating elements that keep reappearing. To me, that was a step forward. That was Rush progressing and not just staying in the same mould we had cast on *2112*.

The title was a comment on the pointlessness of attaching labels to styles of music, while the cover art (a classic in its own right) was a huge celebration of puns on the word 'waves'. It was the first time that humour had appeared on a Rush sleeve, and Hugh Syme unleashed a veritable flood of ideas, one of which included him standing in the background of the picture waving. The main focus is on the Canadian model, Paula Turnbull, who is completely oblivious to the carnage of the storm behind her. There are permanent waves in her hair and a wave to her skirt. In the background, a huge wave crashes over the Seawall Boulevard in Galveston, Texas, during Hurricane Carla in September 1961. A newspaper flaps in the turbulence, with the famous and completely inaccurate newspaper headline from the *Chicago Tribune* advising that 'Dewey defeats Truman'; the two men were opponents in the 1948 United States presidential election campaign. Upon receiving a complaint from the paper, Syme altered it to read 'Dewei defeats Truman'), and later issues of the disc omitted the headline altogether.

Permanent Waves demonstrated that the band was distilling their music into more streamlined compositions without a dip in either the quality of lyrics or musicianship. Integrity forms an overarching theme through the songs, but the point is not rammed home. The traditional tropes of prog rock are still present, but these are not employed for their own sake. *Permanent Waves* is also short; its six tracks come in at under 36 minutes. As one of the first albums to be released in the new decade, it is an indication of the style that would be a near constant of the band's future output. It was also a vital 'bridging' album, setting them on course for the second major musical landmark of their career and subsequent future.

In *Limelight – Rush In The '80s*, Terry Brown said:

> They came very well prepared for that album, with a lot of preproduction. They had spent an inordinate amount of time rehearsing, so they came to the table with things finished, as it were. We didn't spend as much time together as they spent together preparing the songs. That was a big change. It was a fun record, but it wasn't easy. It was hard from a playing standpoint, but again, they were really starting to push the envelope as players.
>
> When they came up with the material for *Permanent Waves*, it was pretty exciting because it was so different. But I hadn't had the conversation, 'We need to come up with something shorter, more concise, or different.' *Hemispheres* was a hard record to make, and it drained everybody creatively, so it seemed only natural that the next record was going to be quite different. You couldn't do two of those in a row.'

'The Spirit Of Radio' (4.56)

In the *Classic Rock* interview, Geddy said:

> That was the song that sparked most of that album from that point of view. We were able to throw a lot of different things into that song in five minutes, and it worked. Music was changing, and radio was changing. Our access to great music – the way we were getting it on FM radio, for example – was dying and becoming more commercialised.' The Spirit Of Radio' carries that feeling, and I think that people related to that song because of the way the music industry was going. It wasn't about love and getting laid, the typical rock stuff. So it was fresh. And there's a very positive sound to that song as well. There's a life to it.

One of the first songs to be written and the first to be recorded for the album, 'The Spirit Of Radio' sees 'prog' collide head-on with radio-friendly rock in an outstanding and accessible opener. The fabulous flanged, rotating guitar riff, intended to replicate the sound of a listener spinning the radio dial through various stations, hits the ears with a breathlessness that still impresses. Powerful blasts of bass and drums are underpinned by a sustained synth. The tempo accelerates into a rising riff that isn't a million miles away from the Zeppelin influences of the debut album.

Twenty-eight seconds in, the lyrical style of the 'new' Rush sound arrives in style with the first verse: 'Begin the day with a friendly voice, a companion, unobtrusive'. Clearly, we are not in *Hemispheres* any more. The title was taken from the slogan of a radio station popular in Toronto, CFNY. The lyrics are a commentary on the shrinking number of radio stations who were prepared to play what they wanted to play, a reaction against the increased commerciality of the medium. It is an interesting metaphor for the band's early struggles as well.

After the second verse, the opening riff returns over a new, repeating, three-quaver pattern: 'Invisible airwaves crackle with life, bright antennae bristle with the energy'. Like much of the song, there is a perfect synchronisation between the energetic, optimistic music and the elegant precision of the lyrics. The third verse heavies up the musical accompaniment and has one of the killer stanzas of the album: 'One likes to believe in the freedom of music, but glittering prizes and endless compromises shatter the illusion of integrity.'

The second chorus is quickly followed by a hard rocking instrumental section (2.54 – 3.33) where Lifeson's emphasis is on chordal shadings, underpinned by bars of 7/4 and 4/4 time. A simple synth melody line appears. There isn't a guitar solo in its 'traditional' place, another sure sign that Rush were, like it or not, moving in a new direction of their choosing.

A brief reprise of the introduction leads into the second surprise. Probably channelling the first (of what would turn out to be frequent) influences of The Police, the coda section is sung over a relaxed reggae feel featuring Erwig Chuapchuaduah on steel drums. An extract of the lyrics of 'The Sound Of Silence' (Simon and Garfunkel, *Wednesday Morning, 3am,* 1964) is re-written to read, 'For the words of the profits are written on the studio wall, concert hall echoes with the sound of salesmen'. At 4.19, Lifeson is finally let off the leash with a furious wah-wah enhanced solo; the song concludes with the rising riff, a further quick flash of the opening ostinato and an aggressive power chord.

'The Spirit Of Radio' is a fantastic track, a regular concert opener, a fan favourite, and an indication that the 'new' Rush was just as adept, agile, and aggressive as the 1970s version. In *Limelight – Rush In The '80s*, Geddy recalled:

> It worked. I don't know whether it was just a relief for people not to have to sit through 25 minutes to get to the end of a song, but we just took all our

> ability and all that experimenting we'd done and focused it in a smaller time period, and the songs really had a lot of power. 'Spirit Of Radio' proved to us we could take a five-minute format and make it complex and make it melodic and make it all work, so that was a big learning moment for us.

'Freewill' (5.21)

This is another cracker. Clear yet complex, intelligent but still involving, the lyrics are again on point, culminating in a compelling chorus: 'You can choose a ready guide in some celestial voice. If you choose not to decide, you still have made a choice. You can choose from phantom fears and kindness that can kill. I will choose a path that's clear, I will choose freewill.'

'Freewill' follows a more conventional structure than its predecessor: an introduction, verse, pre-chorus, chorus, and repeat, with an instrumental in the anticipated place. It's what's going on behind the scenes that adds much to the music.

Starting (and finishing) with a straightforward quaver run down of a C major scale in 4/4, the memorably melodic verse riff alternates between 6/4, 7/4, and 4/4. The pre-chorus is in a rock-solid 4/4, while the chorus moves between three bars of 4/4 and a single bar of 3/4. But none of this seems unnatural or irritating; it's not to misquote 10cc, 'prog for prog's sake'. The strength of the composition is in its melodies, which shine through consistently.

It's the instrumental section (2.50 – 4.01) where the band's true prog colours are unfurled; four bars of 5/4 time truncate the verse melody on guitar and bass, the two bar 4/4 introduction is reprised, and then a glorious section opens up as the time moves into a more flowing 6/8. Here, Lee unleashes a magnificent funk-meets-jazz-rock bass riff against a single sustained synth note. Not to be outdone, Lifeson joins in with what sounds like a concerted attempt to break the neck off his guitar. Notes are wrenched every which way, furious salvoes of rapid phrasing explode, and the sense of a superb guitarist firing off fretboard pyrotechnics at will is joyous.

Lee goes stratospheric for the final pre-chorus ('Each of us, a cell of awareness, imperfect and incomplete. Genetic blends with uncertain ends on a fortune hunt that's far too fleet') before descending to his usual range for the final chorus, the song coming to a close on a sustained G major chord.

'Freewill', like 'The Spirit Of Radio' before it, would become radio and concert staples. They would also feature prominently on the band's numerous live albums and, here's the kicker, never sound dated. Rush's ambition is fully realised in these two songs. Whilst the remainder of this album is more disparate, this pairing shows the trio hitting their preferred target immediately, combining power, intelligence, 'chops' and brevity with an apparent ease bordering on insouciance.

'Jacob's Ladder' (7.26)

In an interview with *Modern Drummer,* Neil said:

> We wanted to build a song around the phenomenon called Jacob's Ladder, where the rays break through the clouds. I came up with a couple of short pieces of lyrics to set the musical parts up. We built it all musically, trying to describe it cinematically as if our music were a film. We have a luminous sky and the whole stormy, gloomy atmosphere, and all of a sudden, these shafts of brilliance come bursting through.

The song title also comes from the Old Testament story of Jacob seeing angels ascend and descend the shafts of light between Heaven and Earth.

The outlier of the album 'Jacob's Ladder' is a studious throwback, sounding more like an escapee from *Hemispheres* than this refreshed, streamlined version of the band. It is a multi-faceted piece which moves through many textures and moods. Unusually, the music was completed first. Peart's minimal, evocative lyrics focus on two of his favourite themes: the elevation of the individual and the power of natural phenomena. His words were added more as an additional texture than the central focus of the composition. Lee and Lifeson's music is magnificent, dramatic, evocative, melodic and powerful; the sense of an approaching storm and the subsequent appearance of the titular phenomena is superbly crafted.

The frequently changing time signatures and repeated low register riffs are highly effective at conveying the approaching storm. The introduction (0.00 – 0.46) features bars alternating between 5/4 and 6/4 while a relentless bass riff, military-style drumming, and a pretty, chorused guitar ostinato work together with a single, unifying synth note. The first vocal section (0.47 – 1.19) is controlled and anticipatory, the underlying syncopated riff relentless, as it builds to a crescendo with the lines 'Thunderheads are rumbling in a distant overture ...'

The next three minutes are entirely instrumental, opening with a heavy chord sequence over which Lifeson adds a melodic lead line before ascending skywards with his soaring solo. The guitar melody returns before an increasingly powerful section, all distorted chords, bass, and drums in a powerful unison rhythm. A synth melody is added on top as the music slowly builds to a climax with repeated D major chords played in quavers over a 3/4 time signature. This fades as the synthesizer proceeds to take centre stage.

Here, the mood becomes more tranquil and free. Devoid of a specific rhythmic backdrop, the simple melodies ebb and flow, decorated with some subtle bell percussion. Lee's effects-processed voice reappears, as if from above: 'All at once the clouds are parted, light streams down in bright unbroken beams.' The contrast between the distorted guitars of the 'storm' section and the refreshing, sunlit keyboards is superb.

The track then enters its second substantial instrumental (4.31 – 6.50) but now with a more positive mood. A low register guitar ostinato in 6/8 and 7/8 begins with the synth playing the 'sunlight' vocal melody. Bass and drums join, the atmosphere builds and builds, the guitar tone becomes more prominent and Peart becomes increasingly busy. The music suddenly climaxes with some furious 4/4 bars where a powerful triplet pattern leads into the final vocals: 'Follow men's eyes as they look to the skies. The shifting shafts of shining weave the fabric of their dreams.' The synth provides the final climatic notes and as these fade, the introductions riff can be heard quietly in the background; another storm is never far away.

If 'Jacob's Ladder' had featured on any previous Rush album it would probably have been expanded further, possibly enough to fill most of an entire side of a record. The fact that the band were consciously working towards a greater economy means that, although this piece is still the longest continuous composition on the album, there is no lessening in the flow of creativity.

'Entre Nous' (4.36)

'Entre Nous' is a companion song to 'Circumstances' from *Hemispheres*, a short, punchy, and direct melodic rocker, which opened side two in the days of vinyl. It's another excellent example of the band's desire and ability to write compact yet still involving songs. This is one of Peart's first forays into writing about relationships, and his words still resonate on this evergreen subject: 'We are secrets to each other, each one's life a novel no one else has read'.

Musically, the introduction and verses are straightforward; a groove is set up in 4/4, utilising some interesting chord inversions. A single bar of 3/4 leads into the chorus (which will also feature in this section), where a 12-string acoustic guitar has prominence, the overall sound becoming heavier for the final lines: '...leave room for you and I to grow'.

After a short reprise of the introduction, the next verse ('We are strangers to each other, full of sliding panels, an illusion show') has a 'half-time' feel. The second chorus is followed by an instrumental section (2.36 – 3.37) where, rather than a guitar solo, Lifeson emphasises the arpeggio patterns of the introduction, extending them further. This technique is particularly effective at 2.50, 3.01, and 3.06. Over this, Lee overlays a simple synth melody, which curls back into the third verse ('We are islands to each other, building hopeful bridges on a troubled sea'). A final chorus and the song finishes on a sustained G major chord, ending on a positive point: 'The spaces in between, leave room, for you and I to grow.'

'Entre Nous' is an overlooked jewel. Rarely performed live, it is still a fine testament to excellent lyrics and confident musicianship wrapped up in a gem of a song.

'Different Strings' (3.48)

'Different Strings' is another 'album-only' ballad, never intended for live performance. The shortest and most straightforward track on the album is another relationship song.

Lee is in fine, gentle voice over Lifeson's graceful arpeggios, especially with the chorus: 'All there really is, the two of us. And we both know why we've come along. Nothing to explain, it's a part of us, to be found within a song.' Guest pianist Hugh Syme's contributions add subtle colour.

At 1.24, bass and drums join this atmospheric mood, with some strange, 'Necromancer'-esque sounding phrases from Lifeson in the background. A second verse and chorus is followed by the highlight of this song; an achingly emotive, bluesy solo where the guitarist uses space around his evocative phrases to fantastic effect. Regrettably this fades far too quickly; I would like to have heard far more of this 'stretching out' against the languid, moody backing.

'Different Strings' is a fine example of the 'less is more' approach. Each instrument has an important and clear part to play and the space around their individual sounds adds to the haunting, melancholic atmosphere.

'Natural Science' (9.20)

Peart had been working on another extended piece for the band based around the story from the 14th century, the time of King Arthur, entitled 'Sir Gawain And The Green Knight'. As he was writing it, he began to realise that 'Sir Gawain' was feeling out of place within the band's new musical direction, and the lyrics were set aside, never to see the light of day again. In Sir Gawain's place, new ideas began to take shape, eventually becoming 'Natural Science'.

This colossus was, therefore, the only track the band didn't have fully arranged and practised before decamping to Le Studio. Another hint of 'The Necromancer' springs to mind with the composition. While 'Natural Science' is the longest track on this album, it is still presented as three separate songs, which segue into each other to form a single piece. There is a lot going on musically, while the lyrics introduce and develop the theme of interactions between humanity and nature as metaphors for relationships between people. Presented as the album's 'epic' in the new Rush universe, it is shorter, less indulgent, and more straightforward while still referencing the familiar stylings of prog rock.

I: 'Tide Pools' (0.00 – 2.21)

The first song is itself in two parts. Initially, we hear the sound of trickling water, recorded *a la' Kings', au naturelle,* using the lake outside Le Studio with an additional, uncredited seagull on backing squawks. Lifeson's dreamy 12-string acoustic strumming and Lee's reverb and delay-enhanced vocals create an intimate yet slightly surreal mood. The lyrics describe the creation of pools by a receding tide, which Peart sees as 'a simple kind of mirror to reflect upon our own, all the busy little creatures chasing out their destinies. Living in their pools, they soon forget about the sea ...'

At 1.46, we move back inside the studio, with a pretty arpeggio guitar pattern and a punchy entry of bass and drums as the music becomes more urgent: 'Wheels within wheels in a spiral array, a pattern so grand and complex. Time after time, we lose sight of the way our causes can't see their effects.' The ostinato pattern becomes more intense, and a sudden electronic effect, akin to a vortex, launches us into ...

II: 'Hyperspace' (2.22 – 5.08)
...which starts with a ferocious rock workout in 7/8 time based around a relentless quaver-based riff. Here the vocals are treated with reversed reverb to give a futuristic, automated effect to match the lyrics. These reflect upon the dangers and benefits of invention and technology in the right (or wrong) human hands. This section is musically brutal, heavy, and unrelenting. There is a sense of relief when, at 2.56, the pulse drops to 4/4 for sixteen bars, and a synth melody takes centre stage over the busy rhythm section.

At 3.19, we're back into 7/8 manic heaviness with some cutting lines: 'Computerised clinic for superior cynics who dance to a synthetic band. In their own image, their world is fashioned, no wonder they don't understand'. A short, spectacular drum fill transports us back to the more melodic 4/4 section, where Lifeson throws in an unusual, wild, and possibly improvised solo (4.08 – 4.31). This slides effortlessly into a new, yearning melody and a reprise of the 'Wheels within wheels' section from 'Tide Pools', only this time with considerably more musical urgency. Two sustained chords herald the conclusion to this section and the introduction of ...

III: 'Permanent Waves' (5.09 – 9.17)
... with Rush wrong-footling the listener again. Instead of continuing the complexity, the title track opens with a four-to-the-floor stomping chord sequence. Soon lurching into a triplet feel, Peart makes his case for a life to be lived in balance: 'Science, like nature, must also be tamed, with a view towards its preservation. Given the same state of integrity, it will surely serve us well.'

There is a celebratory feel here; Rush view the future with guarded optimism. This mood is emphasised still further (7.19 – 7.41) with a fantastic, upbeat chord sequence and a very active drummer. The song concludes with a reprise of 'Wheels within wheels' theme, but this time maintaining the triplet feel and changing the words to 'Wave after wave will flow with the tide, and bury the world as it does. Tide after tide will flow and recede, leaving life to go on as it was.' A crushing coda of chords concludes the song, to be replaced by the sound of ocean waves, providing a neat symmetry with the opening.

While 'Natural Science' moves through many different moods and textures it's the intelligent lyrics which provide cohesion. Peart's contention that 'the most endangered species, the honest man – will still survive annihilation' indicates his emergence as a writer with a gift for the impressive use of language and ideas.

Reviewing the album for the UK music magazine *Record Mirror* at the time of its release, Malcolm Dome said:

> .... Geddy, Alex, Neil and co-producer Terry Brown (almost the fourth member of the band these days) deliver a set of six modern, battle-hardened epics which exhibit enough technical proficiency to satisfy Yes fans, contain sufficient lyrical talking points to win over Floyd freaks, yet never become overbearing or stifling. I strongly recommend those who think intelligent heavy metal is the figment of a half-crazed reviewer's warped sense of humour to get hold of a copy of the album and surprise their ears.

Related Recording

That wasn't it for Rush on record in 1980. Anthem label mates and occasional Rush support act Max Webster released their fifth and final studio album, *Universal Juveniles,* later that year. One track featured all three Websters (Kim Mitchell – guitar and vocals, Gary McCracken – drums, Dave Miles – bass, with former keyboard player Terry Watkinson returning for the session) and all of Rush. It was recorded live at Phase One Studios in Toronto on July 28, with both bands playing the song in the studio at the same time.

Rush fans should seek out further material from this remarkable, if sadly relatively unsuccessful, band. All of their back catalogue (*Max Webster* (1976), *High Class In Borrowed Shoes* (1977), *Mutiny Up My Sleeve* (1978), *A Million Vacations* (1979) and the post-break-up compilation *Diamonds Diamonds* (which included two 'new' songs) are worthy of serious investigation). Subsequently, Kim Mitchell (chief songwriter) went solo (some of which involved Pye Dubois as lyricist), and many of his albums are full of excellent melodic rocking gems. A gifted, distinctive vocalist, his fluid guitar style and intrinsic sense of melody provide many highlights in a decades-long, multi-album career.

'Battlescar' (Mitchell, Dubois) (5.51)

'Battlescar' is an absolute monster of a song. Mid-paced, relentlessly heavy, and performed with complete conviction, it is essential listening for any heavy rock fan. The combination of the two bands playing simultaneously is sonically crushing, and there is a palpable sense of enjoyment at the sheer might of the music the seven players collectively produce. This is highlighted in the memorable chorus: 'Bust the busters, screw the feeders, make the healers, feel the way I feel.'

Each player has the chance to shine; Mitchell and Lee share and trade vocal duties; Lifeson and Peart's distinctive styles are clearly in evidence, but there is no way that the Websters are anything but equal partners in this enterprise. It's not to be listened to at high volume if you're suffering from a hangover, but it's absolutely worth it in any other circumstances.

Moving Pictures

Personnel:
Alex Lifeson: electric and acoustic guitars, Moog Taurus pedals
Geddy Lee: vocals, bass, bass pedals, MiniMoog, Oberheim polyphonic, Oberheim OB-X, Moog Taurus
Neil Pear: drums, timbales, gong, bells, glockenspiel, wind chimes, bell tree, crotales, plywood
Hugh Syme: synthesizer ('Witch Hunt')
Recorded at Le Studio, Morin Heights, Quebec, Canada
Produced by Rush and Terry Brown
Released: 12 February 1981 on Mercury Records
All music composed by Lee & Lifeson with lyrics by Peart, except 'Tom Sawyer' (lyrics by Peart and Dubois)
Chart positions: Canada: 1, US: 3, UK: 3

If *Permanent Waves* was the touch-paper, then *Moving Pictures* was the flame that sent the band rocketing skywards. *Permanent Waves* had shown that shorter songs could lead to greater radio play and exponential growth in popularity without compromising the integrity of the music. With *Moving Pictures*, Rush did what they did before, only better (in the main).

A 96-date *Permanent Waves* tour ran from January to June 1980, with some live recordings being made in Scotland and London for a proposed second live album. Rush, however, wanted to make another studio album. The band's relentless schedule of touring, writing, and recording meant that new material was already in progress. Typically, pieces would be developed during sound checks. Like 'Gawain' before it, a new song based upon Thomas Hardy's 'Wessex Tales', was dropped in favour of the more forward-looking, thinking, and sounding 'Vital Signs'.

After the tour, the band reconvened at Stony Lake Farm, Ontario, to finalise ideas. At the end of August, Rush moved into Phase One studios in Toronto to record demos, and in October, Le Studio again became their 'office'. While still keeping pace with the fast-moving developments in keyboard technology, the band were happy to use such sounds as supporting textures within the power trio framework. The album was recorded with state-of-the-art digital equipment; Terry Brown seemingly matching the trio's constant wish for experimentation and innovation, rather than just treading water and issuing an album which didn't *progress*. In the *Classic Rock* interview, Alex's view was:

> Most of that record was written by all of us at the same time, in the room jamming with an idea and everybody going from there. What we ended up with was, I think, some of the strongest and most enduring material that we've ever written. There are a lot of songs on that record that reached a really high standard.

While *Moving Pictures* is a continuation of Rush's musical journey, cruising closer to the commercial mainstream, there is no loss of central values. The songs are lean, well-structured, and played with a zest, which is still apparent decades later. On its release, rock radio took to the album – well, the first side at least; side two is more 'interesting' – in their droves. The fact that five of the seven songs clocked in at around the four-and-a-half-minute mark meant that it was much easier for programmers to feature the band. In *Limelight – Rush In The '80s*, Alex commented on the idea of the songs as a series of short cinematic experiences:

> Instead of one story, you had five stories in the same time span, but you could link them with a sentiment or with an idea. A little bit less so with *Permanent Waves* but more so with *Moving Pictures*. That whole idea of a collection of short stories is what we were after, and that's what *Moving Pictures* is.

The album title was an apt choice. Syme again pulled out all the stops with another superb and now iconic cover; it's a colour photograph of some picture movers moving three paintings, with the entire front scene being revealed on the back as a scene for a motion picture. The location was the Ontario Legislative Building at 111 Wellesley Street West, Toronto, the seat of government in Ontario. The paintings were of a pretend Joan of Arc, 'A Friend in Need' (a group of dogs playing poker) by C M Coolidge and a red-on-black representation of the 'Starman' from *2112*. The entire image is framed in black with the band's name in a stark, red font. The inner sleeve, still all black, showed the lyrics and other details in white, with three individual black-and-white photos of the band playing their instruments, all captured via slow-motion exposure. More pictures of movement. Syme would later go on to win his first Juno Award for cover art with this sleeve.

The stratospheric success of *Moving Pictures* was as transformative for the band's fortunes as the arrival of Peart in 1974. That said, whilst I prefer *Permanent Waves* as a whole, the first four tracks on this album are absolute, peerless musical magic. Four timeless classics in a row is a triumph of songwriting, performance, production and sequencing. All four would be a near-constant feature, to varying degrees, of every single concert and live album thereafter. And why not? 'Tom Sawyer', 'Red Barchetta', 'YYZ' and 'Limelight' are beyond compare; you'll do a lot of listening before you hear – if you hear – four more perfect examples of brilliant rock music back to back.

Whilst I enjoy the three songs of what, in olden times, made up side two, I find the flow of the album to be disrupted. 'The Camera Eye', whilst being generally excellent, takes up too much time. 'Witch Hunt' is malevolent magnificence, of course, but the unexpectedness of 'Vital Signs' seems designed to shake things up. Of course, what fans didn't realise at the time was that we were witnessing Rush's continual desire for progression being played out in real-time with the album's closing track. As would be seen, 'Vital Signs' would not be a one off. Not everyone approved.

'Tom Sawyer' (4.33)

Whether it's the snarl of the Oberheim synth, the precision drumming, the 'mean, mean stride' of the tempo, the crystal clear vocals, or the might of Lifeson's power chord riffs, the opening section of 'Tom Sawyer' sums up everything that is great about this song, and the album overall. In *Contents Under Pressure,* Geddy reflected upon the iconic track:

> I love that song and I never get tired of playing it. The fact that it is so popular still just confuses the hell out of me. To me, the song is just about innocence more than anything, and I think that comes through. And it still holds through somehow; the slightly inscrutable lyrics still deliver that message to people, and people identify with it, and they dig it. And it's got this weird middle part. And if you can get away with that in a popular song – geez, it's a major victory.

Lyrically, this was the first collaboration between Peart and Max Webster's wordsmith, Pye Dubois (christened Paul Phillip Woods). It was his poem 'Louis the Lawyer' which served as the basis for Peart's depiction of a cynical outsider; the drummer draws parallels between the song's anonymous character ('Today's Tom Sawyer') and that of the titular character of Mark Twain's 1876 novel. In *Contents Under Pressure,* Neil described the collaboration of two very different writer's styles:

> Pye's method is that he just kind of sends me pages of scribbles, and I impose order on them. So, it's a perfect meeting of personalities in that he dwells in an imagistic universe and an impressionistic universe and expresses it as such, whereas I live in a much more ordered universe and impose that structure and rhythm and parallel construction on it. I think right from that foundation, it's a collaboration of personalities as much as it is of words

The song's four vocal sections provide a neat symmetry, each one possessing its own individual, melodic and heavily rocking core:

1: 0.00-0.12: 'A modern day warrior…'
2: 0.13-0.48: 'Though his mind is not for rent…'
3: 0.49-1.10: 'What you say about his company…'
4: 1.11-1.24: 'The world is, the world is…'
1: 1.25-1.34: 'Today's Tom Sawyer…'
5: 1.35-2.32: 'Instrumental'
2: 2.33-3.08: 'No, his mind is not for rent…'
3: 3.09-3.30: 'What you say about his company'

4: 3.31-3.44: 'The world is, the world is...'
1: 3.45-3.57: 'Exit the warrior...'
6: 3.58-4.33: 'Play out'

Taut, muscular and full of swagger, 'Tom Sawyer' is still fresh, exciting, and impressive today. The guitars sound magnificent, the bass work is inventive, while Peart's drumming explains why he topped so many music magazine polls as 'Best Rock Drummer'. Another factor in the song's sonic success is that, until the instrumental section, the pulse remains resolutely in 4/4 time, the vocal melody and chord progressions both being more than strong enough to dispense with any beat displacement.

Come the instrumental section the band slip effortlessly back into their prog-kimonos. A simple descending synth melody is played ten times over 7/8 time, with Lifeson then taking the reins with another fine example of his apparently random, ad-hoc style. Against the clockwork-like precision of Lee and Peart, his seemingly improvisatory phrases provide an impressive counter-balance. There is no lack of thought or technique here; there is a jazz player's technicality to the solo, which benefits from the added sonic effects a highly overdriven electric guitar can bring to the texture. The solo climaxes at 2.23 with repeated high screams, leading to a spectacularly heavy replaying of the synth melody on guitar and bass as Peart pulverises his kit. The reprise of the opening guitar sequence has examples of truly jaw-dropping drumming in the spaces in between the chords. And all of that in just over a minute. Welcome to the new Rush. The play-out section reverts to 7/8 with the synth taking centre stage as the guitar, bass and band riff away relentlessly in the background as the music fades.

In the *Classic Rock* interview, Geddy recalled:

> The hardest thing of all was getting the right guitar sound in the solo section. We wanted that section to be played pretty much as a three-piece, not a whole lot of overdubs, but with a sound that filled up the stereo spectrum and didn't sound empty. The guitar sound for Alex's solo was really critical. It wasn't drowning in echo. We were going for this dry sound with that unique tone, and for it not to feel empty, that was kind of hard. At one point, I said, "We always have one song on every album that doesn't quite click.' And we thought that 'Tom Sawyer' was going to be the one. This just goes to show you we don't know what we're talking about!

'Tom Sawyer' is, for many, the definitive Rush song. It combines a typical lyrical theme (the celebration of individualism) with an intoxicating mix of rock power trio and synth to produce an instant classic. Any track that mixes groove, chops, melodic hooks, and an anthemic vocal with an intelligent perspective was always going to be well received. 'Tom Sawyer' showed Rush were already at another level and weren't content with staying there.

'Red Barchetta' (6.09)

Once described by Lee as 'a pivotal song', the second longest song on the album, 'Red Barchetta' doesn't *feel* excessive due to the exuberance of the playing, the highly charged, melodic sections, and the involving tale. The song is close to perfection with its blend of story, numerous contrasting musical sections and extraordinary musicianship.

'Red Barchetta' is set in an Orwellian-style future where personal transportation has been prohibited. The first-person hero of the tale takes his uncle's 'brilliant red' car from a 'better, vanished time' from a farm into the countryside, where he encounters two government enforcement vehicles. A chase ensues with the narrator escaping via a bridge which proves too narrow for his pursuers. He ends his day back at the farm, dreaming of possibilities with his uncle 'by the fireside'.

Inspired by a short story, 'A Nice Morning Drive' by Richard S. Foster, published in 1973, Peart alters some details for his version. Foster's choice of car (an MGB Roadster) becomes a Ferrari 166MM Barchetta in the drummer's hands. Whereas Peart's hero escapes, Foster's character crashes into a tree as the pursuing vehicles collide, rather than ending up stranded.

Fading in with some delicate guitar harmonics and sustained synth, a pastoral mood is created. A brief bass melody leads into the main driving rhythm. There is a spaciousness to the texture; the chorused guitar is cleanly picked, and bass and drums have 'air' around their sound, giving the music a positive, sunny atmosphere highlighted by Lee's folksy singing style.

Things pick up for the second half of the verse with syncopated stabs from bass and drums until, at 1.13, a fantastic, distorted guitar riff bursts in. This develops into something even better at 1.26 with the type of swinging chord sequences made for head-banging, bringing the excitement level up still further to match the vocals: 'Jump to the ground as the turbo slows to cross the borderline, run like the wind as excitement shivers up and down my spine.'

The tension grows with the music and lyrics in perfect sync as the vocals conclude with 'Fire up the willing engine, responding with a roar, tyres spitting gravel I commit my weekly crime…' And we're off to the races with the next section, which is exhilarating; higher-pitched guitar chords punctuate the relentless bass and drum rhythm. The excitement is palpable, and the music is a perfect backdrop for the tale: 'Wind in my hair, shifting and drifting, mechanical music, adrenalin surge…'

Lifeson's subsequent solo (3.22 – 3.44) is another demonstration of his skill; melodic and yet wild, odd intervals briefly emerge as his phrasing rushes headlong into the 'headbangers delight riff' ™, quickly to be joined by Lee's continuation of the chase: 'Suddenly ahead of me, across the mountain side, a gleaming alloy air car shoots towards me two lanes wide. I spin around with shrieking tyres to run the deadly race, go screaming through the valley as another joins the chase.'

Of note here is how this 'second verse' section sounds so incredibly heavy in comparison to its predecessor. Lee's voice is in full rock mode by now, the band pushing the song to its climax as the hunted escapes, followed by a relaxing conclusion. The final minute, an extended reprise of the opening, features a longer bass solo over Lifeson's arpeggios, with drums and synth a constant presence. A calming guitar melody takes over as the song fades away.

'YYZ' (4.24)

In the *Classic Rock* interview, Geddy remembered that 'YYZ' had an easy gestation:

> Alex wasn't around. Neil and I just went out to the barn at Le Studio, where the gear was set up, and we started putting 'YYZ' together as a bass and drum jam song. Then Al came in and added his licks, and before you knew it, the song was finished.

In contrast to the manic sprawl of 'La Villa Strangiato', 'YYZ' is a firmly focused instrumental which compresses plenty of ideas and a fantastic groove into its four-and-a-half-minute duration.

The opening sequence is based upon the rhythm of the Morse Code call sign for Toronto's Pearson International Airport, YYZ. Initially played on hand cymbals, the band then develop the theme around a note of C and its diminished fifth interval, G flat, in 10/8 time for nine bars, the tenth bar being a series of syncopated power chord stabs. A brief pause is followed by a blistering run of semiquavers at a faster tempo, signalling the end of the introduction.

The main riff (0.43 – 1.10) sets 'YYZ' properly in motion and is, to my mind, a verse melody. It alternates between the underlying chords of F sharp minor and A minor at a still faster tempo. Set in 4/4 time and 16 bars in length, this section is both rhythmically straightforward and melodically complex. The 'chorus melody' (1.10 – 1.37) has a more hopeful quality, rising over a repeated B and C major chord sequence.

Keeping with the previous rhythmic template this becomes a new section where Lifeson moves to a chordal accompaniment for three bars, the fourth being given over to Lee for a single unaccompanied bar of bass solo. The next four-bar phrase has Peart taking this solo slot. This pattern is repeated and then played a further time with both Lee and Peart's contributions having a two-bar duration. Not to be outdone Lifeson's chord work constantly shifts rhythmic shape in the build-up to the brief solo flurries.

The guitarist comes into his own with his stunning solo (2.23 – 2.51). Twisting and turning, fluid and flowing, he makes full use of a guitarist's toolbox of techniques (slides, hammer-ons, pull-offs, bends) to which the whammy bar is frequently used and abused. The four-bar phrases are amusingly punctuated by what sounds like breaking glass but is, in fact, Peart hitting a piece of plywood against a stool. Lifeson's solo is reminiscent of the work of the jazz-rock style of Allan Holdsworth and is regarded as a career highlight, culminating in an excellent two-bar section of descending semiquaver hammer-on/pull-offs. This falls into a new section (2.52 – 3.20), which has a more relaxed, half-time feel with the synthesizer dominating.

Finally, the 'verse' and 'chorus' melodies are reprised, with the track coming to a tight end after a brief restatement of the introduction's theme. 'YYZ' remains the gold standard of advanced technique for guitarists, bassists and drummers the world over.

'Limelight' (4.19)

Reflecting in the *Classic Rock* interview on the pressures of fame, especially on Peart, Geddy said:

> It was at a time when the band was becoming more popular. It was a different level of fame, and Neil was being confronted with things on a regular basis that were making him really uncomfortable. So he wrote that lyric: 'I can't pretend a stranger is a long-awaited friend.' That song was Neil's way of trying to sort it out.

Peart's aversion to the media and fan attention that being a rock star entailed, along with his longstanding desire for privacy and isolation, is given full rein in this confessional lyric. He avoids any 'woe is me, here I am, a famous and respected rock musician trapped in a situation I've worked very hard to get into, and I'm finding it difficult' type naval-gazing by the use of the third person singular ('one') rather than the first person ('I') narrative throughout the song. Even this simple narrative device provides a degree of separation between the listener and the writer.

The first twelve seconds of the introduction riff sound like 'Limelight' is going to be a generic, arena-style clap-a-long contrivance. Once the rhythm section kick in, the track slips into 7/4 time and immediately sounds more authentic, with the synth providing background colour. The verses are underpinned with shifts between 3/4, 4/4, and 2/4 time, with Lee giving an evocative voice to Peart's musings.

The combination of music and lyrics is sublime, none more so than with the classic line 'I can't pretend a stranger is a long-awaited friend'. The chorus is particularly effective, starting in a relatively relaxed state: 'Living in the limelight the universal dream for those who wish to seem …' before becoming more drivingly rocky: 'Those who wish to be must put aside the alienation, get on with the fascination, the real relation, the underlying theme.'

Truly excellent while all this is, the highlight is, again, Lifeson's other-worldly solo (2.37 – 3.19). Initially graceful and relaxed, it builds in ever-increasing anguish, climbing the fretboard in a sequence of arpeggios before finally disappearing with a single, sustained high note. It's another masterclass, seemingly never settling and yet compelling in its construction and execution. In *Contents Under Pressure,* the guitarist offered up his opinion of his work:

> The solo in 'Limelight' is probably my favourite solo to play, and if I feel I've really got the fluidity nailed then it's very, very satisfying personally. The whole thing is just very elastic, and it's not always easy to get everything to be very circular from one part to the next. But when it happens, it's really a treat.

Repeated choruses lead into a big, no, make that *massive* rock ending, with Peart unleashing a superlative lengthy run around his kit before the final power chord.

'The Camera Eye' (10.58)

The mood changes dramatically for what was the second side of the vinyl release, with the apparent abandonment of the concision of the first four songs, allowing the band to stretch out in this tale of two cities. Like 'Xanadu' before it, 'The Camera Eye' is fundamentally the same song played twice. The mood here is one of introspection, with the lyrics offering a detached, almost alienated view of city living. Peart is suggesting that city dwellers should escape the shackles of their environment and appreciate the rest of the world around them.

'The Camera Eye' was to be the last 'long' (exceeding ten minutes) song by the band, and, as such, becomes the outlier on an album where the compositional focus established in the first four tracks is dissipated. Given the amount of time the song takes to actually get going, it's always struck me as a shame that the band didn't apply some vigorous editing to convey the lyrical and musical ideas in a more concentrated form. If the focal length of 'The Camera Eye' had been reduced, a further short(er) song could have been featured on the album, giving a greater sense of balance and cohesion between the two sides of the original vinyl.

Instead, the track takes its time. City noises, sustained synthesizer, and agitated, military-style drumming in the background set up an inherent tension with isolated guitar contributions. Gradually, the texture builds, finally kicking into a steady 4/4 groove at 1.34. Sweeping guitar and synth chords dominate until the mood brightens at 2.21 with a faster keyboard sequence. Guitar, bass, and drums invade this with power and precision before Lifeson introduces the main, magnificent guitar melody.

At 3.31, a poppier-sounding chord sequence appears over which the vocals finally begin. Peart's abilities to convey great detail with few words are in evidence here: 'Grim-faced and forbidding, their faces closed tight, an angular mass of New Yorkers'. These are people who 'chase through the streets of Manhattan', pausing only at a traffic or pedestrian light before continuing their 'flow through the streets of the city.'

At 4.41, a more relaxed mood is established with an effective, repeated guitar arpeggio. The crowd seem 'oblivious to a soft Spring rain, like an English rain.' Amidst the 'buildings lost in a limitless rise', Peart still feels the 'pulse and the purposeful stride', concluding that while New York presents both possibilities and realities, 'the focus is sharp in the city.'

Six minutes in, and we go over to our London correspondent. The same musical framework acts as a canvas for superb lyricism: 'Green and grey washes in a wispy white veil, mist in the streets of Westminster. Wistful and weathered, the pride still prevails, alive in the streets of the city.' The reprised softer section at 8.30 sees the Londoners oblivious to 'a quality of light unique to every city's streets.' Despite 'teeming with intense energy', London is 'calm in this violent sea'.

At 9.18, and somewhat unexpectedly, Lifeson enters from stage left with another searing, melodic solo. Initially not over-playing, he gradually introduces greater complexity and speed, culminating in a dazzling semiquaver display before giving way to the postscript to the track; again, 'the focus is sharp in the city.'

Impressive, descriptive and yet overly unnecessarily long, 'The Camera Eye' dissipates much of the energy displayed with the preceding four songs. Yes, it 'works', but it would have benefited from some substantial editing.

'Witch Hunt' (4.44)

Writing in the *Moving Pictures* tour programme, Peart said:

> 'Witch Hunt' was the winner of the most rewritten song award, being very difficult to get a handle on. But our intention has always been to use it as the 'production number' of the album, in the tradition of such pieces as 'Different Strings', 'Madrigal', and 'Tears'. It would serve as a sort of vehicle for experimentation and indulgence. For instance, we would be using Hugh Syme's talents on the keyboard, and my entire drum part was recorded twice (as two drummers) in the verse, while in another, a percussion section was created by recording each sound differently. The introduction was a very strange endeavour, as we assembled a 'Vigilante Choir' out in the snow and the sound of the haunted child at the beginning.

The third part of an anticipated trilogy of songs focusing on fear, 'Witch Hunt' seethes with malevolence and bile. A musical retelling of the 1940 novel *The Ox-Bow Incident* by the American writer Walter Van Tilburg Clark (1909 – 1971), Peart describes the mentality of the mob. There is no let-up or resolution to the song; unremittingly bleak and disturbing, the music is similarly relentless and tense.

Over an aggressive playing of a child's toy (the hint here being that hatred is a learnt behaviour, rather than an inherent, biological trait), a dystopian minim-based riff (G, G an octave above, D flat, D, A, B flat, G flat) is heard against a backdrop of wind chimes and the voices of an angry crowd. This threatening mood is added to by a menacing-sounding synth, and the volume increases to breaking point.

At 1.05, a fresh, faster G minor-based riff is unleashed: 'The night is black, without a moon, the air is thick and still. The vigilantes gather on the lonely torch-lit hill'. A new chord sequence appears over the same claustrophobic tempo, led by the synthesizer, and more lyrics warning against the group actions of people driven by an overbearing sense of their own morality. This is best displayed in the killer lines 'They say there is strangeness too dangerous in our theatres and bookstore shelves. Those who know what's best for us must rise and save us from ourselves.'

The finale to the song ('Quick to judge, quick to anger, slow to understand, ignorance and prejudice and fear walk hand in hand') is backed by a mighty sounding synth, the song grinding to its slow end with the sound of a church organ briefly appearing at the close.

Advances in technology meant that the band *could* replicate the song in its sonic entirety, and as soon as 1984's *Grace Under Pressure* tour, the song was in the live set.

'Vital Signs' (4.46)

In *Contents Under Pressure,* Geddy remembered the song's gestation:

> Usually, on every album, there's one song that we write spontaneously, just at the last minute, and that's the one for that album. And those songs usually end up taking us in a totally different direction, as that one did. It's kind of a precursor for us getting more involved with sequencers. I love those last-minute ones because you write them and record them in a short period of time, and it ends up being a lot of fun.

That Rush were not content to sit on their substantial laurels was immediately clear here. The band felt they needed a very *different* type of song with which to end the album. Seeking an up-tempo piece with more of a relevant, modern commercial feel to it, they came up with this divisive tune. A sonic curved ball for fans, married to lyrics which display a world of possibilities for the creative individual, 'Vital Signs' is a Rush song like no other thus far. It would prove to be a significant pointer for the music the band would produce for part of the new decade. Peart's theme, that technology, rather than dominating human existence, might well mimic our inherent nature, thus remaining under our control, is set against a blend of reggae and new wave textures.

Clean guitars chop between channels, a sequenced synth sample bubbles away, and a medium tempo sets the scene for the reverb-treated vocals:

'Unstable condition, a symptom of life, in mental and environmental change.' Things kick up a notch 48 seconds in with a simple chugging and overdriven guitar rhythm where 'the impulse is pure' but 'sometimes our circuits get shorted by external interference.'

The obvious influence of The Police is present throughout, with only the unique vocabulary and distinctive vocals reminding the listener that this is Rush. 'Vital Signs' is both an optimistic end to the album and a signpost to the band's future. They were intent on progressing, and the hope was that their fan base would follow them. And, if they didn't, new fans would join in their wake.

The play-out (3.22 onwards) is the song's lengthy low point. Over a relentless, repeated descending chord sequence, Lee riffs on variations of the lyrics, with exhortations that 'everybody got to deviate from the norm'. Or 'elevate'. Or 'escalate'. Interest wanes, and the fade doesn't come soon enough.

The song left some perplexed fans in its wake. Was 'Vital Signs' a one-off, an anomaly? Or the band's future? All would be revealed some eighteen months later, and those hoping for a *Moving Pictures 2* were going to be sorely disappointed. The synths were on the rise, Lifeson would be in retreat and the songs would be less 'prog meets rock' and 'more prog encounters pop, ska and reggae, goes on a date and decides to make a go of it'. In *Contents Under Pressure,* Alex reflected on the changes that the album meant for the band:

> When *Moving Pictures* came out ... that was really the big turning point. We were still in debt up to this point. And it wasn't until *Moving Pictures* came out that we could actually get ourselves out of debt. We went to the next level of playing big gigs and more radio airplay, specifically with 'Tom Sawyer' and 'Limelight'.

And in the *Classic Rock* interview, he summarised:

> The songs were good. They connected with a bigger audience. But there was also something about the sound of that record that resonated with people. *Moving Pictures* was very successful. It's no exaggeration to say that this record changed our lives.

Exit – Stage Left

Personnel:
Alex Lifeson: electric and acoustic guitars, synthesizers, bass pedals
Geddy Lee: vocals, bass, synthesizers, bass pedal synthesizers, occasional rhythm guitar
Neil Peart: drums and percussion
'A Passage To Bangkok', 'Closer To The Heart', 'Beneath, Between And Behind' and 'Jacob's Ladder' recorded at The Apollo, Glasgow, Scotland (June 1980)
All other songs were recorded at The Forum, Montreal, Canada (March 1981)
Mixed at Le Studio, Morin Heights, Quebec, Canada
Produced by Terry Brown
Engineered by Paul Northfield
Released: 29 October 1981 on Mercury Records
Chart positions: Canada: 7, US: 10, UK: 6

Prior to the issue of *Exit Stage Left,* Mercury's German operation released a single, 'picture disc' compilation album, *Rush Through Time,* in 1979. This incurred the displeasure of the band and the wrath of their management company. *Rush Through Time* was fundamentally a reissue of the Mercury US DJ-Promotion disc *Everything Your Listeners Ever Wanted To Hear By Rush But You Were Afraid To Play.* This had been released in 1976 as a taster for radio stations in an attempt to get the band greater airplay.

The reissue dropped two songs from *Caress Of Steel* in favour of two tracks from *A Farewell To Kings.* The album was subsequently repackaged as a standard vinyl album with a colour sleeve and updated graphics on the back cover in 1981. The track listing was 'Fly By Night', 'Making Memories, 'Bastille Day', 'Something For Nothing', 'Cinderella Man', 'Anthem', 'Overture'/'The Temples Of Syrinx', 'The Twilight Zone', 'Best I Can', 'Closer To The Heart' and 'In The End', all of which were taken from the studio albums

Rush's second double live album established the format for the band's career up to 1997: four studio albums followed by a live release. Recordings gathered together during the *Permanent Waves* and *Moving Pictures* tours of 1980 and 1981, respectively, were used for the band's next release.

Following the end of the *Moving Pictures* tour, the band returned to Le Studio and sifted through over 50 reels of tape recordings. The aim was to find the absolute best of the individual song performances and touch up any mistakes using preferred extracts from other recordings. This search for sonic perfection, the reduction in crowd noise, and the curious decision to largely present songs with fades of audience approval rather than a continuous listening experience rob an extremely strong set of material of its inherent 'liveness'. Allowing 'perfect' to be the enemy of the 'good' creates a relatively sterile record, which is quite the achievement given the material on display.

Of course, no album is *truly* live; there is always the desire to present the best possible version of a band to its actual and potential fan base. As any musician knows, mistakes go with the territory, and even more so when putting forward energetic, technically complex performances. The temptation to paper over the cracks is too great, and Rush succumbed to this to a degree to rival Judas Priest's 1979 live album *Unleashed In The East* (amusingly renamed *Unleashed In The Studio* by its critics) and UFO's seminal *Strangers In The Night* (1979), where two whole tracks were re-recorded back in the studio, with the appropriate crowd noise being added later on.

The title is taken from the catchphrase of Snagglepuss, a cartoon character from the Hanna-Barbera stable. Whenever he got into trouble the pink puma could be heard to utter 'Exit stage right' or *Exit Stage Left* as he left the scene. 'Stage left' is a theatrical direction for actors; the left-hand side of the stage is that of the audience, not the performers' perspective. In *The Art Of Rush,* Neil said:

> We wanted the tail from Snagglepuss, the old cartoon movie, because the phrase *Exit Stage Left* comes from him. We wanted just a little pink tail in that image. But, you can imagine, the corporations getting all corporation-y!

Syme's cover is a magnificent creation. The viewpoint is backstage with characters from all the band's previous studio albums waiting to 'go on'. Paula Turnbull (of *Permanent Waves* fame) is pulling the large green curtain aside to allow us a view of a packed auditorium, golden light cascading down onto the empty stage, two microphone stands and some of the band's stage equipment being visible. The 'stage' part of the cover was from an actual Rush concert in Buffalo Memorial Hall, Buffalo, New York, while the 'behind the scenes' aspect was photographed at the (then abandoned) Winter Garden Theatre in Toronto.

To Paula's left, the businessman from Hemispheres looks ill at ease, as well he might as the snowy owl from Fly By Night is flying above his bowler-hatted head. The puppet monarch of *A Farewell To Kings* slumps over a box emblazoned with the logo from the band's debut, his crown on the floor. Behind him, a picture of the red Starman and pentagram from *2112* on a black background is visible. Two men dressed in red overalls wait to move a fully framed image of 'The Necromancer' (*Caress Of Steel*) while a naked Dionysis of *Hemispheres* fame strikes a pose in the far left.

On the inner red sleeve, and in complete contrast to the multiple images of the band presented with *All The World's A Stage*, there are three individual photos of the trio in live performance. Lifeson is mid-power-chord, the stage lights reflecting off the front of his guitar to create an explosive effect. Peart is shot from beneath and behind and at an angle, his impressive array of percussion instruments again bathed in golden light. Lee has an altogether moodier look; shot in silhouette against a night sky lighting, he is clearly involved in the music. No faces are visible. This emphasises the notion that the band's increasing fame was causing them to put more distance between themselves and their fans. Laughably, my copy of the disc has the performers' pictures reversed; both Lifeson and Lee are now left-handed players!

As with *All The World's A Stage,* there is a short paragraph from the band to the listener:

> Well, just a few more words! In seven years of touring, we have made many friends in many different places. Some have worked for us, some have cheered for us, and some have just been nice to us.' For reasons beyond our comprehension, we have become increasingly more popular and hence stretched ever more thinly among even more people. If sometimes we can't give the time to our friends and loved ones, we hope they will understand and forgive us. After all, we didn't change, everybody else did!'

'The Spirit Of Radio' (5.11)

As if to emphasise the patchwork approach to the album, there is a quick fade in of crowd noise; Lee briefly introduces the song and a high-energy rendition of the best track on *Permanent Waves* kicks proceedings off. A few seconds of crowd approval swiftly fades out.

'Red Barchetta' (6.46)

'This is a song about a car; this is 'Red Barchetta', intones Lee, and the familiar introduction sets forth. As with 'The Spirit Of Radio', this is performed with panache, accuracy, and plenty of live energy, but again, it sounds *so* close to its studio equivalent as to make the listener wonder if they are hearing the original with some added crowd noise. The coda section doesn't, of course, fade, instead coming to a somewhat clumsy (for Rush) conclusion in its final seconds.

'YYZ' (7.43)

The main difference between this and its studio counterpart is the inclusion of a Peart drum solo (2.21 – 5.22), which appears immediately before Lifeson's solo.

'A Passage To Bangkok' (3.45)

A welcome inclusion of one of the frequently overlooked tracks on the second side of *2112,* 'A Passage To Bangkok' is suitably mighty in a live situation. Lee's high-pitched vocals sound like he's enjoying singing this one. He provides rhythm guitar behind Lifeson's solo, the bass notes also being played by him on synthesizer pedals.

This song was omitted from the first issue of the album on CD due to the time constraints of the medium at the time. The re-issue series rectified this error as technological advances had found an extra five minutes of running time for the discs, probably down the back of the sofa.

'Closer To The Heart' (3.08)

The second song from the Glasgow section of the album features a crowd sing-a-long, which earns them a sleeve credit: 'A special tribute to the Glaswegian Chorus for the background vocals on 'Closer To The Heart'. Nice one, folks!' The play-out section, complete with a magnificent drum roll, segues this directly into…

'Beneath, Between, And Behind' (2.34)

…and, suddenly, *Exit Stage Left* sounds like a live album. Taken at a brisker pace than the original, the second verse is omitted, which is a shame, but this is still a compelling and impressive performance of another gem from the band's earliest days.

'Jacob's Ladder' (8.46)

We are treated to the fade-in of a bizarre introduction, a straightforward chord arpeggio progression with simple bass and drum accompaniment, which is, apparently, a short rendition of 'Ebb Tide', a song from 1953 by Carl Sigman and Robert Maxwell. The crowd enjoys it, clapping along as Lee says, 'We'd like to do an old song for you right now. This was done a long time ago by T.C. Broonsie. This is called 'Jacob's Ladder''. The 'Broonsie' is a sideways nod to producer Brown. The song itself is considerably heavier on stage while maintaining its atmospheric mid-section with conviction.

'Broon's Bane' (1.37)

This is a short, nylon-strung guitar piece composed and performed by Lifeson, the title being another doff of the cap to Terry Brown. Relying entirely on arpeggio patterns, it contains elements of both Spanish and jazz genres before segueing effortlessly into the familiar introduction of …

'The Trees' (4.50)

… where the switch between the nylon-strung and the subsequent electric guitar is just a little too smooth and quick to be believed! Otherwise, this is another authentic and enjoyable rendition, the coda section bending into a long, sustained synthesizer note, which becomes the introduction to …

'Xanadu' (12.09)

The live setting allows the trio to stretch out, especially in the lengthy, highly evocative introduction. 'Xanadu' puts any non-fan suggestions that the song couldn't be performed live with such accuracy firmly in the bin. The final power chord is a thing of greatness!

'Freewill' (5.31)

A barely audible count-in unleashes an up-tempo rendition of the second-best song on *Permanent Waves*. The instrumental section is particularly impressive as Lifeson adds even greater pain and speed to his solo, while Lee and Peart deliver the goods with equal relish.

'Tom Sawyer' (4.59)

The concert staple was in its early years at this time; this version stays remarkably close to its studio counterpart. The now familiar live ending makes its first appearance and would feature on most of the live albums the band would subsequently issue.

'La Villa Strangiato' (9.37')

The original classical guitar introduction is replaced by some violined electric guitar and then a plethora (yes, a plethora) of fast phrases. Lifeson's otherworldly mid-song solo is another spectacular highlight.

During the 'Danforth And Pape' section, Lee unexpectedly breaks into a Yiddish rap, which is 'loosely' translated as 'Patty-cake, Patty-cake, Mother's going to buy you new shoes, Father's going to buy you socks, Baby's going to have red cheeks.' Indeed! A brief 'Thank you very much, goodnight' and 'that's all, folks'. In *Limelight – Rush In The '80s*, Geddy remembered:

> That one was an attempt to kind of exaggerate how perfect you could make a live album. There was a lot of meddling with the tapes and trying to make sure we had the best performances. We also made a conscious effort to pull down the audience a bit and emphasise the music. It turned into a bit of a nightmare of mixing and perfecting.

In the same publication, engineer Paul Northfield confirmed:

> They did a lot of repairs on that record because their first live album had been so raw, and they were so uncomfortable with it. They went to the complete opposite extreme on *Exit – Stage Left*. Apart from any drums, they replaced almost everything – vocals, guitars, a huge amount, in order to have more perfection. This actually makes it more of a hybrid; it's like a live bed track album with a lot of overdubs on it.

Signals

Personnel:
Alex Lifeson: electric and acoustic guitars, Taurus pedals
Geddy Lee: vocals, bass, synthesisers
Neil Peart: drums and percussion
Ben Mink: electric violin ('Losing It')
Recorded at Le Studio, Morin Heights, Quebec, Canada
Produced by Rush and Terry Brown
Engineered by Paul Northfield
Released: 9 September 1982 on Mercury Records
All music composed by Lee & Lifeson with lyrics by Peart, except 'Chemistry' by Peart, Lee, and Lifeson.
Chart positions: Canada: 1, US: 10, UK: 3

Moving Pictures put Rush in the big league. Record sales boomed, and an American and Canadian tour sold spectacularly well, all of which enabled the band to renegotiate its contract with Mercury. Further touring in the United Kingdom and America followed, and thoughts turned to the next studio project. There was an implicit obligation to do something different. The band viewed *Permanent Waves* as a 'bridging album' between their long-form full-on-prog-past and the more concise, up-to-date musical stylings of *Moving Pictures*. What they were determined not to do was to fail to progress further.

For Lee, this meant a near-total immersion in the world of synthesisers. The dynamics within the band were changing, with Lifeson's guitar playing more of a supportive role. New material was written, and several songs which would end up on *Signals* were honed during sound-checks for a brief two week 'Tour of the Nadars'. In April, the band headed back to Morin Heights with the new album completed by early July. Rush did not want to repeat themselves; they were confident that they could progress in any musical direction of their choosing. It was essential to them that they did not release *Even More Moving Pictures*.

The recording process proved more wearing than before; keyboards and guitars were fighting for the same sonic ground – the new technology won out. In addition, Terry Brown wasn't particularly enamoured with the results and felt that some of the new compositions were not the band's best work. Fractures in the previously streamlined and breathtakingly efficient Rush machine were beginning to appear. In *Chemistry,* he recalled:

> It was all becoming very electronic. I had arrived at the point where I couldn't contribute more if that was the direction they were going in; it just wasn't my forte. The keyboard thing was becoming overtly the band sound, which I didn't think was cool either. There wasn't a big incident, but I think the writing was on the wall. There were some edgy moments, which were very unusual for us.

In *Contents Under Pressure,* Alex said:

> Certainly, on Signals, there was a conflict, I think, between the guitar and the keyboards we were using. For me that's always been a bit of a sore spot, that record. Because I think there's good material on there, but I think the production on it is lacking. We were just really starting to get into keyboards, and I don't think we were well-balanced on that record. And I think that's part of the reason we had decided to move on, in terms of what producer we were going to work with. We wanted to get a little more of an influence from other people.

The advances in keyboard technology were proving exciting compositional tools for Lee, and the musical world was changing fast, with the new wave, ska, and reggae genres grabbing the limelight. With *Signals*, Rush left behind their unique, established sound and immersed themselves in the incorporation of the popular styles of the era. The end result was a curious hybrid of rock and synth-based pop, with the occasional acknowledgement of their prog preferences of only a few years previous. Fans were, in the main, less than impressed, and as a consequence, the record did not sell as well as its predecessors.

The cover, a bright and amusing image of a dalmatian sniffing a fire hydrant on fake grass, is light, colourful, and a far cry from the sombre, gothic tones of *Moving Pictures*. The rear cover featured a blueprint of a suburban neighbourhood showing imaginary areas and buildings based on the trio's nicknames. The inner sleeve had individual images of the threesome with an added optical pixelation effect. It was all so very modern for the time.

In *Rush – Beyond The Lighted Stage,* Geddy explained the need for a substantial transformation in the band's style and sound:

> We were too curious, we were too dissatisfied with where we were at, and just because we got successful doesn't mean we're going to stop. That's the motivation – we have to find the 'better' Rush.

Signals signalled (sorry) the band arriving at a point of, seemingly, no return. As much as the fans may have wanted them to tread water, the lure of new tech toys and the ever-changing musical world was too strong to resist. While *Signals* is not a 'concept album' *per se*, there is a theme running through it: the life of a man; a childhood in the suburbia of 'Subdivisions', he considers escape as 'The Analog Kid', grows into the 'Digital Man', encounters various types of relationship in 'Chemistry', faces his various demons in 'The Weapon', and emerges as a freshly focussed 'New World Man', before the considerations of older age give pause in 'Losing It'.

The final track, the add-on anomaly, which is 'Countdown', could, in retrospect, be a timely reminder that whatever goes up can and will come down.

'Subdivisions' (5.33)

And so it begins. *Signals* is immediately defined by the full-fat synth riff, which opens 'Subdivisions'. Dark and deep, it's an impressive introduction but it also sets the entire tone of the song and a lot of the album. Just imagine how much more effective the opening chord sequence would have been if Lifeson had played it with a distorted tone, with the main melody then being added on the synth over the malevolent 7/4 rhythm. Still, we are where we are, and the guitarist's role throughout this song and across the following tracks is more textural than commanding.

That typed, 'Subdivisions' is the first of only four really good songs on the album. Despite the aural misgivings, the lyrics are excellent, homing in on the alienated, creative individual who can't or won't fit into various social groups. Peart introduces a surely, part-autobiographical element here: 'Growing up it all seemed so one-sided, opinions all provided, the future pre-decided, detached and sub-divided in the mass production zone. Nowhere is the dreamer or the misfit so alone', a feeling that is crystallised with the line 'be cool, or be cast out.'

Despite Lifeson's apparent relegation, he still has some opportunities to shine; the chiming arpeggios in the chorus chime brightly, and at 4.20, he plays a highly processed yet still strongly melodic solo. But he is fighting for space with the synth. Other affecting moments include Lee's relaxed, folksy vocals, which carry the line 'Somewhere out of a memory of lighted streets and quiet nights...' with conviction, and Peart's spoken word performances of the title in the choruses.

On the negative side, the tempo is unrelenting; there is very little by way of dynamic or textural alteration, and the synth dominates throughout. There is not much technical virtuosity on display here and the overall sound is mid-rangy and, ultimately, suffocating.

Perhaps this was deliberate, the mix of the instruments a musical expression of the dullness of suburban living, but as an opening track for an eagerly awaited album, 'Subdivisions' is good, but not great. Put up against 'The Spirit Of Radio', or 'Tom Sawyer', it feels distinctly 'mid-side' in quality. Acceptable and enjoyable, it lacks the killer combination of power, melody, and invention which marked out its predecessors as classic Rush compositions. Despite its relative sonic flabbiness, the song was performed frequently and would feature on many of the band's subsequent live releases. The reason 'Subdivisions' works is down to the connection it makes with the listener. Geddy expanded on this in *Limelight – Rush In The 80s*:

> It was all about where we came from and what we escaped. That's the strength of the song and what gives it enduring resonance for so many people in so many different countries. There are so many people who came out of the suburbs and know that feeling, know what kind of cultural wasteland it looks like and smells like, and that song really hit it for them. It

wasn't the first song of Neil's that resonated with me, but it was a shift because it was the first one that spoke more directly about where we all come from. And for that reason, it's quite different. It's a song about alienation.

'The Analog Kid' (4.47)

Things move up several gears with this energetic, driving rocker. 'The Analog Kid' is a song about the desire to explore, and its energy level matches this wish. The introductory guitar riff is superb, the tempo is fast and exciting, and Lee gives a good, clear voice to the lyrics.

It was all going so well. Then, at 1.04, the speed slows, the synth awakes, and excitement is dissipated for the next 40 seconds as the texture is set to 'extra mush'. The chorus lyrics, however, remain sharp as the young narrator thinks about cities with 'your buildings and your eyes, autumn woods and winter skies' and an 'open sea and city lights, busy streets and dizzy heights.'

The opening riff and rocking groove return, and Lee's voice builds spectacularly through the lines, 'The boy lies in the grass, unmoving, staring at the sky. His mother starts to call him as a hawk goes soaring by. The boy throws down his baseball cap and covers up his eyes. His higher range is perfect for these final few words. It also sounds like, for the first time on the album, he is truly invested in Peart's character.

And again, as night follows day, the tension is quickly spent, and the synth raises its head again for the 'You move me, you move me' chorus. Luckily, the power is turned back on again for the denouement, with the final lyrics underlying the character's need to explore the world around him: 'When I leave I don't know what I'm hoping to find, and when I leave I don't know what I'm leaving behind…'

Then, and it's a truly joyous moment, Lifeson's lead guitar grunts, growls, wakes up and swings into hyperbolic action as he unleashes a ferocious solo, his contribution possibly enhanced by his frustration at the role he had to play in the band mix. The closing section is repeated with a salvo of the opening riffs, bringing this fine track to a close as the synth bubbles away to silence.

Subsequent live recordings of 'The Analog Kid' would give the song the sonic rebalancing it needs here. The absence of an acoustic guitar for the softer sections is, to my ears, a mistake. Imagine a chiming 12-string guitar and, possibly, a piano underpinning the 'You move me' moments contrasting with the savage rock trio explosion. Perhaps that was a suggestion that Terry Brown might have made, only to be overruled as the synthesisers assumed control.

'Chemistry' (4.57)

A three-way lyrical collaboration with Lee and Lifeson throwing in their ideas for Peart to give final shape to, 'Chemistry' comes across as banal wordplay which analyses the processes of the world and the many types of connection that can be made. Yes, it's as dull as I've described. And musically, it's not much better.

The 'Chemistry' lesson starts well. An anthemic opening with synth and guitar again joined in battle soon settles into a comfy, mid-tempo groove. Lifeson has some impressive, repeated high-pitched semi-quaver runs before Lee gets started on 'Signals transmitted, message received. Reaction making impact, invisibly'. You see what I mean? Luckily, this is all sung over a refreshing, guitar-led, and relatively rocking (for this album) chord progression. Come the pre-chorus, the synth and a clear Police influence appear, building to a climactic chorus of 'Electricity? Biology? Seems to me it's Chemistry'. Apparently, an alternative line, 'English Literature, can be a bitch to yer', was considered but wisely discarded.

'Chemistry' isn't a bad song, *per se*. It just doesn't go anywhere or do much, seemingly being content to orbit around its collection of reasonably adequately melodic ideas. There are many elements interacting here, but the resultant combination is not a success.

Lifeson has a squealy, tortured solo four minutes in, which shows he has lost none of his creative skills, and this is the best section of the song. The track could have been developed better as an instrumental, possibly titled 'Why, Why Bother?' During an interview for the radio premiere of the new album, Neil said:

> That was the mish-mash approach to trying to take diverse influences and make them work together. It starts out basically as a hard rock trio, then goes into a ska or reggae style of rhythmic approach, then it has sort of a modern European contemporary approach to the sequencer chorus and then goes right back down to a basic trip again for the instrumental section, and then builds up through the changes again. It's all very confusing!

Yes, it is. You can add the words 'unfulfilling', 'disappointing' and 'a missed opportunity' into that analysis as well. Sadly, 'Chemistry' would never receive the sort of proper, heavy redemption that the similarly underwhelming 'Digital Man' would get treated to on 2008's *Snakes & Arrows – Live* album. Somewhere in here is a semi-decent song trying to escape, but there's too much going on for genuine fulfilment.

'Digital Man' (6.20)

Hope springs eternal. What does the 'Digital Man' have to offer? Not much, as it turns out. Faster of tempo with a spirited drum introduction, Lifeson and Lee soon begin busying themselves. The words tell of a man of science, apparently separated from the passions of nature, who wishes for something more, a life beyond mere factual information. The chorus is the most telling part of the lyric: 'He'd love to spend a night in Zion, he's been a long while in Babylon, He'd like a lover's wings to fly on, to a tropic isle in Avalon'.

At this point, the 'progressive reggae', which has been wafting around parts of the record, comes into its own. A companion song to 'The Analog Kid', the verses here have a greater musical power than the ska-based chorus, which is starting to feel like the band's new default setting. At 2.50, the mood shifts again, becoming more powerfully four-square as Peart surmises that the Digital Man still has 'a date with fate in a black sedan.' The Analog Kid is now an adult, doing his best to get ahead and not lose his race to the rats of 'Subdivisions'. But death awaits us all, including him.

The truly irritating thing about these 'lesser' songs on *Signals* is the fact that you *know* that the band can do better. The influence of The Police again looms large behind Lifeson's inventive solo section (3.23 – 4.32). A reprise of the chorus leads again into the 'black sedan' progression, with the song fading as Lee repeats the lines, 'He plays fast forward for as long as he can, but he won't need a bed, he's a digital man'. His voice eventually drops into speaking the refrain (possibly out of boredom), which slows as the song fades.

'Digital Man' is too disparate. There's a sense of 'everything and several kitchen sinks' being thrown at it. The underlying musical ideas are reasonable, and there are moments where the ears think, 'This is going to kick into something really good soon'. Mixing reggae, ska, synth-pop, and rock must have seemed like a good idea at the time. Sadly, the lobes, by and large, remain underwhelmed. In *Chemistry*, Terry Brown remembered his dislike of the composition:

> I wasn't crazy about it; it had that sort of Police thing going, and it didn't really sound like Rush. But you know it was a tune; I had to make it work; let's get on with it; let's do it as well as we could. I think we did a good job of it, but it was a little odd.

'The Weapon' (6.23)

And so it continues. Subtitled 'Part II of 'Fear'', 'The Weapon' is nowhere near as good as 'Witch Hunt', not by a long chalk. Again, the synth leads the way and needs to shoulder much of the responsibility for this ... mess. Over a steady yet inventive drum pattern, Lifeson introduces a Celtic-themed ostinato before some actual power chords ring out as the vocals begin. Lyrically, 'The Weapon' focuses on how governments and religions of all hues use their powers to subjugate people, best summarised with the couplet 'And the things that we fear, are a weapon to be held against us.' Worthy words indeed. If only Lifeson and Lee had written music to match the mood.

The opening line, 'We've got nothing to fear but fear itself?', is the famous quote of the United States President Franklyn D. Roosevelt, turned upside down by the addition of a question mark. Peart asks why we should not also be scared of pain, failure, tragedy, and breakdowns, both mechanical and emotional. We then encounter a man of integrity who is 'not afraid of your judgement, he knows of horrors worse than your Hell.' He's 'a little bit afraid of dying, but he's a lot more afraid of your lying.' The backing is stronger here, although the emphasis is on pop melody rather than raw rock power.

Whereas 'Witch Hunt' was compelling, dark, and threatening, a perfect foil for some of Peart's most incisive writing, here we have a bizarre mixture of electronica-based disco with some rock thrown in, almost as a sap to long-time fans. The atmosphere is almost jovial, bouncing along merrily and out of step with its lyrical content. In *Limelight – Rush In The 80s*, Neil remembered the song as…

> …an interesting exercise in juxtaposition. I had these really doomy, black images in there and Geddy had written a lot of the musical sections for it at home as a sort of electro-beat, modern dance exercise. We weren't sure we'd ever use it. Now, because Geddy has to sing the words, a lot comes down to the decisions he and I make. He persisted with his idea that we should approach the treatment again from a really abstract point of view, juxtaposing his electronic dance music with the dark, doom-laden lyric of mine, and making it work somehow. And I think we did. I'm really glad it took the brooding, heavy quality away from the lyrics.

And therein lies the problem. I have nothing against electronic dance music; it's just not my thing. Much more importantly, it just doesn't work here. 'The Weapon' falls well short of the mark and it is the music which is at fault. Peart's work deserves better and doesn't receive it. This mistake would be repeated with 'The Enemy Within' on 1984's *Grace Under Pressure*. The trilogy was thought to be complete. However, by the time of the 'comeback' album – *Vapor Trails* in 2002 – the concept would be expanded to a tetralogy with the addition of 'Freeze', which sadly won the prize, even beating 'Didacts And Narpets' for the band's least enjoyable composition.

The lengthy, ambient instrumental section (3.22 – 5.14) wanders around aimlessly between the speakers in search of some inspiration. Lifeson throws in some isolated, distorted phrases before getting into a solo which screams away in the distance. This builds to a climax, which then dissipates into a morass of synth and drum fills. 'Integrity Man' turns up briefly again before the end of this too-long song, which finally fades away, with Lifeson's Celtic melody making a re-appearance amidst the synth and drums.

I am not, generally, one to write a song off on the basis of a single listen, especially a Rush song, given the amount of thought, time and care that has gone into the composition, performance and production. Despite repeated listens, each time with hopeful, open and fresh ears, 'The Weapon' remains a dud, an unexploded bomb that was poorly manufactured and should never have landed on this album.

'New World Man' (3.42)

Written quickly to bring the album up to an appropriate running length and originally referred to as 'Project 3.57' for precisely that reason, 'New World

Man' is a welcome blast of fresh air, pulsing with energy, melody and top-notch performances.

The 'New World Man' is 'old enough to know what's right, but young enough not to choose it.' Here, he is ready to face challenges, driven to become better than he was. And as long as he learns from his mistakes there is no doubt, in Peart's mind, that he will prosper.

Of course, this being 'new' Rush, the synth is never far away. 'New World Man' works because the band here starts to sound more like their true selves. Under time pressures to get the track completed, they dispense with any frills and get straight to the musical point. This is underlined best in the superb, up-tempo chorus, which dispenses with The Police influence, which, yet again, dominates the verses. The band's attempts to sound like the English pop-reggae trio would lead some to suggest Rush should rename themselves 'The Mounties'. Lee's harmonised vocals are excellent, the music drives along relentlessly, and the melodic power is undeniable.

Bereft of any solo section, this, the album's shortest song, could have done with further development. Trim *at least* two minutes from 'The Weapon' and there would be more space to explore the ideas here. As it is, 'New World Man' is, after 'The Analog Kid', the best song on the album. In *Limelight – Rush In The 80s*, Terry Brown ruminated:

> Deep down inside, my thoughts were, 'Why are you doing this?' The Police are doing it so well themselves; why are we doing it? But we pursued it, and we made it unique enough that it has some interesting parts. And lyrically, it has substance. It was a hard one for me to get my head around. It just seemed an odd way to go. I'm not really a big reggae fan, so that also affected the way I thought about it.

He makes a good point. 'New World Man' works because it is compact, powerful and melodic. There isn't any 'fat' to be trimmed here, and if this song had been the only one to dip its toes in reggae's waters, then it would be a refreshing diversion.

'Losing It' (4.52)

The album's ballad, and also the track that most engages the band's prog settings again, 'Losing It' is an absolutely superb mixture of haunting melodies and considered lyrics. We encounter an ageing dancer ('stiff as wire, her lungs on fire' after a practise session, she 'limps across the floor and closes her bedroom door') and a writer who 'stares with glassy eyes' at his 'empty page', his mind 'dark and dulled by sickness and indecision'. Peart is in top form here, creating two worlds with an impressive economy and his gift for the well-chosen word.

Musically, 'Losing It' is just as good. The repeated quaver-based ostinato in 5/8 time is reminiscent of a dancer with 'her aching limbs and downcast face aglow with perspiration' relentlessly practising her moves with diminishing returns, or the tap-tap of a typewriter ('a mechanical device which printed words on the page via the medium of ink, m'lud') as the writer seeks inspiration. The synth works well here creating a hypnotic mood to which the electric violin (played by Ben Mink of the band FM) adds further emotive layers. Writing in the *Signals* tour programme, Neil commented on the inclusion of the guest musician:

> We had talked for a while about getting Ben Mink to play electric violin somewhere on this album, and this seemed like the perfect track. We worked him hard, squeezed him dry and threw him away. Not only the monumentally fantastic solo did we demand, but we had him multiple-tracking an entire string section as well. That'll teach him to be our friend!

Drums, guitar, and bass join in for the 'writer' verse, with the tempo and texture conveying the two artists' worry and frustration that their best days are now behind them. At the two-minute mark, the music becomes stronger, and the song's final lyrics pack the best punch here: 'Some are born to rule the world, to live their fantasies. But most of us just dream about the things we'd like to be. Sadder still to watch it die than never to have known it. For you, the blind that once could see, the bell tolls for thee ...' This line, borrowed from Ernest Hemingway, could suggest that the characters of the song may be considering suicide or that the ever-onward march of time means that there never will be a return to former glories.

The instrumental section is very much Mink's playground, and he acquits himself well against the unsettling 11/8 time signature. Lifeson is also present in the mix, but again, his contribution is textural rather than jaw-dropping. At 3.57, the guitarist assumes centre stage with a revolving riff in 12/8 before the tempo slows, the time switches back to 5/4, and the song fades away as Lee again intones, 'For you, the blind that once could see, the bell tolls for thee...'

'Losing It' is an outstanding song; intelligent and thoughtful lyrics, supremely emotive music and the compelling and considered, rather than screamed, vocals give full voice to thoughts that all creative people must consider as time marches on. The 5/8 time signature gives the music an unsettled yet not disturbing feel, and the inclusion of the electric violin is a flash of genius. The instrument's tone is perfect here; it is a better choice of instrument than the expected distorted electric guitar.

'Countdown' (5.50)

Rush were invited by NASA to attend the first launch of the space shuttle 'Colombia' on 12 April 1981. This song documents the experience, and the track incorporates actual radio footage, as well as sound effects of patrol jets and helicopters amidst the synth-heavy music.

'Countdown' is a dated oddity, a musical commentary of an actual historical event; it's no fan's definition of a classic Rush song. Peart's paean to the astronauts and scientists who made it possible is better read as poetry rather than listened to on the recording. Uncharacteristically, he drops the ball with the line 'Excitement so thick you could cut it with a knife', and then reaches, like the clichéd writer he isn't, for the rhyming of the next line with '...life'.

The music leading up to the actual launch is appropriately taut and tense with anticipation. Power chords scythe through the synth backing, and while this is in 4/4 time, the inventive beat displacements ensure the song doesn't become overly leaden. At the two-minute mark, a synth melody reminiscent of *Permanent Waves* appears for seven bars as the musical power builds towards take-off.

At 2.55, the music swings into a more familiar Rush mode. The time switches to 10/4, with Lifeson's ostinato sounding like it belongs on *Hemispheres* as the countdown continues. Normal service is resumed at 3.12 as Columbia lifts off. What we should hear here is a soaring, celebratory guitar solo as a tribute to the successful feat of engineering taking flight. Instead, we get the bloody synth *again*, which, after the song's final lyrics, doesn't realise that it has outstayed its extremely limited welcome and is back for another go with its cheery 'prog-lite' melody.

In the background, Lifeson patiently plies his way through the chord progression; another opportunity for him to shine wasted. At 5.01, the 'Son of Hemispheres' riff reappears, and the music fades with the sound of the messages between NASA and Columbia as the shuttle accelerates towards the stars. In *Chemistry*, Geddy recalled:

> We felt it was kind of a failure in getting the right balance between synthesiser technology and hard rock. We leaned too heavily into keyboards and ignored the guitar aspect of it.

And, continuing on the subject of Brown's subsequent departure from Planet Rush, he added:

> It really was a necessary thing, not out of any disrespect or any problem in communicating with each other, but a matter of our band falling into a dangerous rut. We wanted to put ourselves in a kind of shock treatment.

In the *Classic Rock* interview, Lee offered the following view of this pivotal album:

> The *Signals* album was a turning point for the band. It was the beginning of our 'keyboard era'. We had used synthesisers since way back, but on *Signals,* that really came to the forefront. *Signals* was a good record, but after that, there was another big change. We decided to go with a new producer. We

didn't want to go back to Terry Brown. We didn't think that was the right thing to do. We were set on moving forward.

Writing in the *Grace Under Pressure* tour programme, Neil recalled the historic parting of ways:

> I guess shortly after the release of *Signals* we began to think and talk of the future. In the early part of the tour, our long-time friend and co-producer, Terry Brown, flew down to meet us in Miami. After the show, riding on our bus through the dark and steamy Florida night, we sat back, drinks in hand, to discuss our future course. Alex, Geddy, and I had been discussing these things for a while now and had decided it was time for us to strike out on our own and try working with someone else. We wanted, no, *needed*, to find out if someone, perhaps from a different background, might have different approaches and different techniques to offer to both our music and our sound.
>
> It was important (and difficult) for us to express to Terry that this in no way signified a dissatisfaction or lack of confidence in him. It was just that after almost ten years and eleven albums together, we had evolved into a comfortable and efficient recording team, the four of us, and we could even pretty well predict each other's opinions and reactions to different ideas. As positive as this situation may sound, this is exactly what we were worried about.
>
> Still, it's no easy thing to tell someone after all this time you want to work with someone else for a change – and still harder to be told it. It was tough for us and it was tough for Terry. We had been through so much together, and he had contributed so much to our development and refinement, both as people and musicians. It was awkward, difficult, and even a bit painful, but we had to do it or wonder, 'what if we had?' While objectively, one may recognise the right thing to do, subjectively, it's sometimes too easy to rationalise the easy way out. We had to cut the umbilical cord.

Peart's words are prophetic. With a now permanently vacant producer chair in the studio, Rush were striking out on their own. In line with their mantra of continual change and progress to find 'the best Rush', Brown would never return to his pivotal role. As a final album together, *Signals* has never been one of my favourites. When it's good, it's very good, but some of the material fails to engage either heart or mind in a positive way. The balance between keyboards and guitar, kept under such eloquently effective control on *Moving Pictures*, feels like a step too far in the wrong direction.

... To Be Continued ...

Nine studio and two double-live albums in less than ten years is an astonishing work rate, especially when factoring in Rush's seemingly inexhaustible wish to tour. *Signals* was a crucial turning point in the band's career. The album saw the end of what many fans who had been with them throughout the 1970s, fondly regard as a 'golden era'.

Music was progressing, technology too was advancing with astonishing speed, and Rush were not going to be left behind. Fearing repetition and stagnation, the albums which followed *Signals* are a mixed bag. That is not to say they don't contain some great songs; each release from 1984 through to their epic finale in 2012 contained some excellent material. Eventually, there would be a return to their natural, organic home – that of the pure, hard-rocking power trio.

Rush 3.0 gave us *Grace Under Pressure*, a mostly solid effort that dialled back the keyboards but was hampered by a sterile clinical production style. 1985 gave us the synth-heavy opulence of *Power Windows,* where the mother of all kitchen sink productions was thrown at some good but mostly unspectacular material. 1987's *Hold Your Fire* continued the softening trend, with the band, to some long-term fans' eyes and ears, an almost unrecognisable shadow of their former selves. This was followed by what was really a 1980s live retrospective with their third double-live album, *A Show Of Hands,* in 1989. In the same year, there was, finally, a partial stripping back to the band's core guitar, bass and drums sound with the relatively weak-sounding *Presto*.

1991's bright and shiny-sounding *Roll The Bones* was another huge seller, even though much of the material presented was merely whelming. A return to a guitar-centric heavy attack with *Counterparts* was welcomed in 1993, and three years later, *Test For Echo* noted a resurgent Rush with plenty still to offer. The band effectively came to an end for five years when Neil Peart's daughter and wife died within a year of each other in tragic circumstances. What was thought at the time to be their final release, a triple live album, *Different Stages,* emerged in 1998.

Fortunately, Rush joined forces again, and version 4.0 released four more studio albums: the powerful and intense *Vapor Trails* (2002), a fun and hard rocking 'covers' mini-album *Feedback* (2004) and an impressively heavy *Snakes & Arrows* (2007). The band finally bowed out of the studio with the magnificent concept album *Clockwork Angels* in 2012.

In the 2000s, the band also released seven (yes, seven) live albums: *Rush In Rio* (2003), *R30 – 30th Anniversary World Tour* (2005), *Snakes & Arrows Live* (2008), *Grace Under Pressure 1984 Tour* (2009), *Time Machine: Live In Cleveland 2011* (2011), *Clockwork Angels Tour* (2013) and, finally, *R40* in 2015.

It's an impressive body of work with, production fashions aside, many great songs nestling alongside some other less-than-inspiring material. Rush finally came to an end with Peart's decision to retire from the band after *R40* due to health issues and his subsequent tragic early death from a brain tumour in 2020. His legacy, and that of the band he transformed, is an inspiring story of three dedicated, hard-working, and supremely talented men who insisted on doing things their way and produced some of the finest rock music to be heard at any time.

Being the arty type, I have always been interested in the visual aspects of the band, especially album covers and band logos. Certain groups have used the same style of name logo for decades to establish their particular 'brand'. Examples include AC/DC, Status Quo, Iron Maiden, Judas Priest, Thin Lizzy and UFO, amongst many others. These designs confirm to the fan exactly what sort of music they can expect to hear. With Rush, that 'style' is more elusive and less predictable.

Whilst certain designs of the band's name have gained traction over the years with the t-shirt-wearing fan base (notably, the debut and 2112), there isn't a single defining Rush logo. Like the music they produced, the band just couldn't be pinned down to a standardised 'look'. Even albums which naturally 'pair together' (*A Farewell To Kings* and *Hemispheres*, likewise *Power Windows* and *Hold Your Fire*) don't share a design consistency. I appreciate that this is a minor point in the grand scheme of things, yet I find it intriguing that every single 'version' (for want of a better word) of the band had a different, constantly changing visual aspect: a perfect mirror to reflect upon the progressive (in the true sense of the word) nature of their music.

A worldwide fan base continues to support the subsequent work of Lifeson (playing guitar as part of the very different, ambient-sounding Envy Of None project) and Lee, who published his autobiography *My Effin Life* in 2023 and supported it with book tours in Canada, the United States and across Europe. Frequently, the author would welcome a 'special guest' to the stage. And, sure enough, Lerxst would appear, a fabulous tribute to a lifelong friendship which has inspired hundreds of thousands of fans in our own lives.

And, of course, as time refuses to stand still, notable dates are commemorated by the 40th anniversaries of landmark recordings such as *2112*, *A Farewell To Kings*, *Hemispheres*, *Permanent Waves*, *Moving Pictures* and, lastly, at the time of writing, *Signals*. Interestingly, these newly remastered versions do not contain any bonus tracks. Rush had a policy of only recording the material they deemed good enough to go on an album. Unlike many of their contemporaries, there were no 'lost tracks', no extended versions and no out-takes. Instead, in addition to new artwork from the ever-prolific Syme and substantial and interesting CD liner booklets, we get some rare, never-before-released live recordings. Only *Signals* bucks this trend with no 'new' concerts to enjoy.

Do these remastered releases sound better than the originals? Well, thanks to advances in technology, yes, of course. But, personally speaking, I would have loved to have heard some material that didn't make it onto the album or versions of songs with different guitar solos, a fresh vocal take or an unexpected tempo change. For example, in the DVD *Classic Albums – 2112 And Moving Pictures*, Terry Brown remembered the problematic nature of finding the 'right' take of 'Tom Sawyer' when listening to the original, well-prepared demo of the now classic track:

> I noticed that one of the big changes in this was the tempo. The demo is quite a few bpm (beats per minute) faster, in fact. It just didn't sit in the groove properly at that tempo ... it just felt that it wasn't 'speaking' properly at that tempo. Singing it at a slower tempo gave the lyrics a little bit more substance. It gives you more time to think about what you're hearing.

Now, that would be something worth shelling out more money for. Other gems could include Lifeson's 'complete' solo on 'Different Strings' from *Permanent Waves* and all of *Signals,* with the focus on the sound of the power trio and the synths relegated to a supporting role. As it is, the anniversary remaster concerts serve as worthwhile reminders of just what a great band Rush were.

There will be a sequel to this book, covering the period 1984 – 2015, where Rush 3.0 and, amazingly, given the tragic circumstances, Rush 4.0 arose from the ashes. That the band continued to produce music of exceptional standards during their renaissance in the 21st century says much about their character. It would have been far too easy to go out and play lots of the old classics just for the money and adulation. Rush 4.0 did not do that. They continued to write and perform high-quality new material and put on some truly amazing shows, some of which have been captured in excellent quality on DVDs which were issued with the various live albums. All of this will be discussed in detail in the follow up book...

The Best Of Brown

What follows is a purely personal 'best of Rush 1.0 and Rush 2.0' for what many fans, myself included, think of as the band's best era. Coming a close second are the excellent albums Rush 4.0 released following their reformation in 2002. Entirely subjective, bound to cause discussion, and putting myself up as a target for derision and criticism, these are the tracks that a 'Best of Brown' era CD should include. Not a great title, I'll admit, but better than 'Top Terry's', which was my first thought.

Taking a single track from each of the 11 official releases between 1973 and 1982, including the first two double live albums, I offer the following as a selection of the band's most essential tracks:

1: 'Working Man' – *Rush*
Well, it had to be the opener. It's one of the reasons Rush managed to get a foothold in the American market, and hence why I came to write this book.

2: 'By-Tor And The Snow-Dog' – *Fly By Night*
The band's first epic track, and an encapsulation of what made Rush such an original and exciting band to teenage rock ears.

3: 'No One At The Bridge' – *Caress Of Steel*
Halfway through the sprawling 'Fountain Of Lamneth' lies this superb track, notable for the range of Lee's vocals and Lifeson's emotive solo.

4: 'Overture' – *2112*
Still blistering after 40 years of listening, 'Overture' is a heavy rock instrumental *par excellence.*

5: 'Bastille Day' – *All The World's A Stage*
Raw, powerful and full of fire, this was the first Rush song I heard on the first Rush album I bought.

6: 'A Farewell To Kings' – *A Farewell To Kings*
I think the title track often gets overlooked, given the colossus that is 'Xanadu', but the song is a brilliant display of writing, technique and performance.

7: 'La Villa Strangiato' – *Hemispheres*
This astonishing *pot-pourri* of ideas from classical, pop, rock and jazz has, as a centrepiece, one of Lifeson's finest solos.

8: 'Freewill' – *Permanent Waves*
One of Peart's finest lyrics is married to great music with excellent results. A concert favourite, this is another timeless classic from the band that could seemingly, at this stage of their career, write them at will.

9: 'Red Barchetta' – *Moving Pictures*

Another 'classic adjacent' song, 'Red Barchetta' captures perfectly the 'story-in-a-single-song' idea the band were aiming for.

10: 'Tom Sawyer' – *Exit Stage Left*

No Rush compilation would be complete without this masterpiece of a composition.

11: 'New World Man' – *Signals*

The only truly successful marriage of the band's reggae influence into their core sound on the album, or any of the others that followed during the 1980s.

Also available from Sonicbond

Horslips – on track

Every album, every song

Richard James
Paperback
160 pages
37 colour photographs
978-1-78951-263-1
£15.99
$22.95

Every album and every song by this cult Irish band.

Five-piece Horslips are arguably the greatest band in Irish rock music history, producing truly special, unique music in the 1970s. By joining literary craft and their cultural heritage with a fusion of traditionally inspired music with rock instrumentation, they created a genre of music which became known as 'Celtic Rock'.

Horslips also pioneered an 'in-house' approach to the rock music business, controlling their stage presentation, graphic design, record pressing and concert promotion. Their finest albums – *The Tain*, and *The Book Of Invasions* – adapted legendary and historic texts with compelling music. Elsewhere the life and times of Turlough O'Carolan, The Famine and emigration provided a conceptual backdrop to *Danceball Sweethearts*, *Aliens*, and *The Man Who Built America*.

But the band broke up in 1980. Reconvening in the next century, after the 'longest tea break in history', they produced a new 'acoustic covers' album, played stadium-filling gigs and television performances, and recorded two live albums. With a foreword by bassist/vocalist Barry Devlin, this book celebrates (and sometimes criticises) the creative waves that Eamon Carr, Barry Devlin, Johnny Fean, Jim Lockhart, and Charles O'Connor gave us

Genesis – on track
Every album, every song

Stuart MacFarlane
Paperback
144 pages
44 colour photographs
978-1-78951-005-7
£14.99
$21.95

Every album and every song by this classic British prog/pop band.

From schoolboy band to sold-out stadium tours and worldwide album sales of over 100 million, Genesis were one of the defining progressive rock bands of the seventies, playing a huge part in shaping the genre. Over a career spanning fifty-five years from formation to the Last Domino? tour of 2021, they developed and adapted through many changes, some of which polarised their existing fans but attracted countless new ones. While *Foxtrot* and *The Lamb Lies Down on Broadway* helped define progressive rock, it was the three-piece line up of Tony Banks, Mike Rutherford and Phil Collins that became the real hit-makers, with albums like *Invisible Touch* and *We Can't Dance* and massive hit singles like 'No Son of Mine' and 'Land of Confusion'.

This book takes the reader on a journey through their entire catalogue, which includes fifteen studio and six live albums, including five consecutive number ones in the UK and five consecutive top tens in the USA, visiting each album in turn and examining every track. It is compiled from the viewpoint of a lifelong fan, and it is hoped that the book stirs many old memories, as it has done for the author, as well as providing some insight for more recent fans of the band.

On Track Series

Allman Brothers Band – Andrew Wild 978-1-78952-252-5
Tori Amos – Lisa Torem 978-1-78952-142-9
Aphex Twin – Beau Waddell 978-1-78952-267-9
Asia – Peter Braidis 978-1-78952-099-6
Badfinger – Robert Day-Webb 978-1-878952-176-4
Barclay James Harvest – Keith And Monica Domone 978-1-78952-067-5
Beck – Arthur Lizie 978-1-78952-258-7
The Beatles – Andrew Wild 978-1-78952-009-5
The Beatles Solo 1969-1980 – Andrew Wild 978-1-78952-030-9
Blue Oyster Cult – Jacob Holm-Lupo 978-1-78952-007-1
Blur – Matt Bishop 978-178952-164-1
Marc Bolan And T.rex – Peter Gallagher 978-1-78952-124-5
Kate Bush – Bill Thomas 978-1-78952-097-2
Camel – Hamish Kuzminski 978-1-78952-040-8
Captain Beefheart – Opher Goodwin 978-1-78952-235-8
Caravan – Andy Boot 978-1-78952-127-6
Cardiacs – Eric Benac 978-1-78952-131-3
Nick Cave And The Bad Seeds – Dominic Sanderson 978-1-78952-240-2
Eric Clapton Solo – Andrew Wild 978-1-78952-141-2
The Clash – Nick Assirati 978-1-78952-077-4
Elvis Costello And The Attractions – Georg Purvis 978-1-78952-129-0
Crosby, Stills & Nash – Andrew Wild 978-1-78952-039-2
Creedence Clearwater Revival – Tony Thompson 978-178952-237-2
The Damned – Morgan Brown 978-1-78952-136-8
Deep Purple And Rainbow 1968-79 – Steve Pilkington 978-1-78952-002-6
Dire Straits – Andrew Wild 978-1-78952-044-6
The Doors – Tony Thompson 978-1-78952-137-5
Dream Theater – Jordan Blum 978-1-78952-050-7
Eagles – John Van Der Kiste 978-1-78952-260-0
Earth, Wind And Fire – Bud Wilkins 978-1-78952-272-3
Electric Light Orchestra – Barry Delve 978-1-78952-152-8
Emerson Lake And Palmer – Mike Goode 978-1-78952-000-2
Fairport Convention – Kevan Furbank 978-1-78952-051-4
Peter Gabriel – Graeme Scarfe 978-1-78952-138-2
Genesis – Stuart Macfarlane 978-1-78952-005-7
Gentle Giant – Gary Steel 978-1-78952-058-3
Gong – Kevan Furbank 978-1-78952-082-8
Green Day – William E. Spevack 978-1-78952-261-7
Hall And Oates – Ian Abrahams 978-1-78952-167-2
Hawkwind – Duncan Harris 978-1-78952-052-1
Peter Hammill – Richard Rees Jones 978-1-78952-163-4
Roy Harper – Opher Goodwin 978-1-78952-130-6

Jimi Hendrix – Emma Stott 978-1-78952-175-7
The Hollies – Andrew Darlington 978-1-78952-159-7
Horslips – Richard James 978-1-78952-263-1
The Human League And The Sheffield Scene –
Andrew Darlington 978-1-78952-186-3
The Incredible String Band – Tim Moon 978-1-78952-107-8
Iron Maiden – Steve Pilkington 978-1-78952-061-3
Joe Jackson – Richard James 978-1-78952-189-4
Jefferson Airplane – Richard Butterworth 978-1-78952-143-6
Jethro Tull – Jordan Blum 978-1-78952-016-3
Elton John In The 1970s – Peter Kearns 978-1-78952-034-7
Billy Joel – Lisa Torem 978-1-78952-183-2
Judas Priest – John Tucker 978-1-78952-018-7
Kansas – Kevin Cummings 978-1-78952-057-6
The Kinks – Martin Hutchinson 978-1-78952-172-6
Korn – Matt Karpe 978-1-78952-153-5
Led Zeppelin – Steve Pilkington 978-1-78952-151-1
Level 42 – Matt Philips 978-1-78952-102-3
Little Feat – Georg Purvis - 978-1-78952-168-9
Aimee Mann – Jez Rowden 978-1-78952-036-1
Joni Mitchell – Peter Kearns 978-1-78952-081-1
The Moody Blues – Geoffrey Feakes 978-1-78952-042-2
Motorhead – Duncan Harris 978-1-78952-173-3
Nektar – Scott Meze – 978-1-78952-257-0
New Order – Dennis Remmer – 978-1-78952-249-5
Nightwish – Simon Mcmurdo – 978-1-78952-270-9
Laura Nyro – Philip Ward 978-1-78952-182-5
Mike Oldfield – Ryan Yard 978-1-78952-060-6
Opeth – Jordan Blum 978-1-78-952-166-5
Pearl Jam – Ben L. Connor 978-1-78952-188-7
Tom Petty – Richard James 978-1-78952-128-3
Pink Floyd – Richard Butterworth 978-1-78952-242-6
The Police – Pete Braidis 978-1-78952-158-0
Porcupine Tree – Nick Holmes 978-1-78952-144-3
Queen – Andrew Wild 978-1-78952-003-3
Radiohead – William Allen 978-1-78952-149-8
Rancid – Paul Matts 989-1-78952-187-0
Renaissance – David Detmer 978-1-78952-062-0
Reo Speedwagon – Jim Romag 978-1-78952-262-4
The Rolling Stones 1963-80 – Steve Pilkington 978-1-78952-017-0
The Smiths And Morrissey – Tommy Gunnarsson 978-1-78952-140-5
Spirit – Rev. Keith A. Gordon – 978-1-78952- 248-8
Stackridge – Alan Draper 978-1-78952-232-7

Status Quo The Frantic Four Years – Richard James 978-1-78952-160-3
Steely Dan – Jez Rowden 978-1-78952-043-9
Steve Hackett – Geoffrey Feakes 978-1-78952-098-9
Tears For Fears – Paul Clark - 978-178952-238-9
Thin Lizzy – Graeme Stroud 978-1-78952-064-4
Tool – Matt Karpe 978-1-78952-234-1
Toto – Jacob Holm-Lupo 978-1-78952-019-4
U2 – Eoghan Lyng 978-1-78952-078-1
Ufo – Richard James 978-1-78952-073-6
Van Der Graaf Generator – Dan Coffey 978-1-78952-031-6
Van Halen – Morgan Brown – 9781-78952-256-3
The Who – Geoffrey Feakes 978-1-78952-076-7
Roy Wood And The Move – James R Turner 978-1-78952-008-8
Yes – Stephen Lambe 978-1-78952-001-9
Frank Zappa 1966 To 1979 – Eric Benac 978-1-78952-033-0
Warren Zevon – Peter Gallagher 978-1-78952-170-2
10cc – Peter Kearns 978-1-78952-054-5

Decades Series

The Bee Gees In The 1960s – Andrew Mon Hughes Et Al 978-1-78952-148-1
The Bee Gees In The 1970s – Andrew Mon Hughes Et Al 978-1-78952-179-5
Black Sabbath In The 1970s – Chris Sutton 978-1-78952-171-9
Britpop – Peter Richard Adams And Matt Pooler 978-1-78952-169-6
Phil Collins In The 1980s – Andrew Wild 978-1-78952-185-6
Alice Cooper In The 1970s – Chris Sutton 978-1-78952-104-7
Alice Cooper In The 1980s – Chris Sutton 978-1-78952-259-4
Curved Air In The 1970s – Laura Shenton 978-1-78952-069-9
Donovan In The 1960s – Jeff Fitzgerald 978-1-78952-233-4
Bob Dylan In The 1980s – Don Klees 978-1-78952-157-3
Brian Eno In The 1970s – Gary Parsons 978-1-78952-239-6
Faith No More In The 1990s – Matt Karpe 978-1-78952-250-1
Fleetwood Mac In The 1970s – Andrew Wild 978-1-78952-105-4
Fleetwood Mac In The 1980s – Don Klees 978-178952-254-9
Focus In The 1970s – Stephen Lambe 978-1-78952-079-8
Free And Bad Company In The 1970s – John Van Der Kiste 978-1-78952-178-8
Genesis In The 1970s – Bill Thomas 978178952-146-7
George Harrison In The 1970s – Eoghan Lyng 978-1-78952-174-0
Kiss In The 1970s – Peter Gallagher 978-1-78952-246-4
Manfred Mann's Earth Band In The 1970s – John Van Der Kiste 978178952-243-3
Marillion In The 1980s – Nathaniel Webb 978-1-78952-065-1
Van Morrison In The 1970s – Peter Childs - 978-1-78952-241-9
Mott The Hoople And Ian Hunter In The 1970s –

John Van Der Kiste 978-1-78-952-162-7
Pink Floyd In The 1970s – Georg Purvis 978-1-78952-072-9
Suzi Quatro In The 1970s – Darren Johnson 978-1-78952-236-5
Queen In The 1970s – James Griffiths 978-1-78952-265-5
Roxy Music In The 1970s – Dave Thompson 978-1-78952-180-1
Slade In The 1970s – Darren Johnson 978-1-78952-268-6
Status Quo In The 1980s – Greg Harper 978-1-78952-244-0
Tangerine Dream In The 1970s – Stephen Palmer 978-1-78952-161-0
The Sweet In The 1970s – Darren Johnson 978-1-78952-139-9
Uriah Heep In The 1970s – Steve Pilkington 978-1-78952-103-0
Van Der Graaf Generator In The 1970s – Steve Pilkington 978-1-78952-245-7
Rick Wakeman In The 1970s – Geoffrey Feakes 978-1-78952-264-8
Yes In The 1980s – Stephen Lambe With David Watkinson 978-1-78952-125-2

On Screen Series
Carry On… – Stephen Lambe 978-1-78952-004-0
David Cronenberg – Patrick Chapman 978-1-78952-071-2
Doctor Who: The David Tennant Years – Jamie Hailstone 978-1-78952-066-8
James Bond – Andrew Wild 978-1-78952-010-1
Monty Python – Steve Pilkington 978-1-78952-047-7
Seinfeld Seasons 1 To 5 – Stephen Lambe 978-1-78952-012-5

Other Books
1967: A Year In Psychedelic Rock 978-1-78952-155-9
1970: A Year In Rock – John Van Der Kiste 978-1-78952-147-4
1973: The Golden Year Of Progressive Rock 978-1-78952-165-8
Babysitting A Band On The Rocks – G.d. Praetorius 978-1-78952-106-1
Eric Clapton Sessions – Andrew Wild 978-1-78952-177-1
Derek Taylor: For Your Radioactive Children –
Andrew Darlington 978-1-78952-038-5
The Golden Road: The Recording History Of The Grateful Dead – John Kilbride 978-1-78952-156-6
Iggy And The Stooges On Stage 1967-1974 – Per Nilsen 978-1-78952-101-6
Jon Anderson And The Warriors – The Road To Yes –
David Watkinson 978-1-78952-059-0
Magic: The David Paton Story – David Paton 978-1-78952-266-2
Misty: The Music Of Johnny Mathis – Jakob Baekgaard 978-1-78952-247-1
Nu Metal: A Definitive Guide – Matt Karpe 978-1-78952-063-7
Tommy Bolin: In And Out Of Deep Purple – Laura Shenton 978-1-78952-070-5
Maximum Darkness – Deke Leonard 978-1-78952-048-4
The Twang Dynasty – Deke Leonard 978-1-78952-049-1

And Many More To Come!

Would you like to write for Sonicbond Publishing?

At Sonicbond Publishing we are always on the look-out for authors, particularly for our two main series:

On Track. Mixing fact with in depth analysis, the On Track series examines the work of a particular musical artist or group. All genres are considered from easy listening and jazz to 60s soul to 90s pop, via rock and metal.

On Screen. This series looks at the world of film and television. Subjects considered include directors, actors and writers, as well as entire television and film series. As with the On Track series, we balance fact with analysis.

While professional writing experience would, of course, be an advantage the most important qualification is to have real enthusiasm and knowledge of your subject. First-time authors are welcomed, but the ability to write well in English is essential.

Sonicbond Publishing has distribution throughout Europe and North America, and all books are also published in E-book form. Authors will be paid a royalty based on sales of their book.

Further details are available from www.sonicbondpublishing.co.uk. To contact us, complete the contact form there or email info@sonicbondpublishing.co.uk